Elementary Poetry
Textbook and Activity Book

by Sonja Glumich

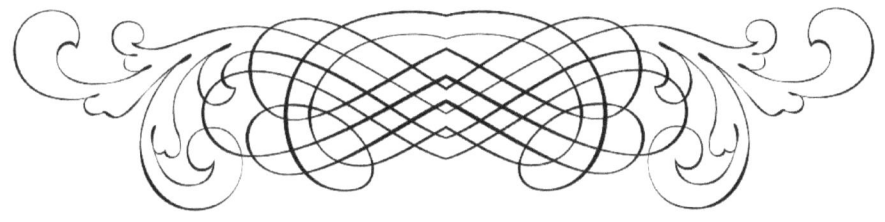

Poetry Study for Elementary School-Aged Children

Volume 3: Poetry of Nature, Revelry, and Rhyme

Interweaves poetry, vocabulary, mapwork, discussion, copywork, recitation, narration, and review questions.

Under the Home Press Division
www.underthehome.org

Front Cover
Original Source: Louey, C. and Dibdin S. (1907). "The Golden Staircase - Poems and Verses for Children." New York: G.P. Public Domain (1907, {PD-US}) This work is in the public domain in the United States because it was published (or registered with the U.S. Copyright Office) before January 1, 1923.

Copyright © 2020 Sonja Glumich
All rights reserved.

No part of this work may be reproduced, scanned, or electronically transmitted without prior permission of the copyright owner unless actions are expressly permitted by federal law the family exception detailed below.

The copyright owner grants an exception for photocopying or scanning and printing pages for use within an immediate family only. Scanned pages should never be used for any other purpose including sharing between families, posting online, transmitting electronically, or resale.

This exception does not extend to schools or co-ops, however a reasonable licensing fee for reproduction can be negotiated by contacting Under the Home, the publisher.

For more information or to report errata, please contact Under the Home at contact@underthehome.org.

ISBN-13: 978-1948783019

DEDICATION

For Chris, Everett, Cassidy, and Calista – my beloved family and curricula test squad.

TABLE OF CONTENTS

POET I: LEWIS CARROLL
Lesson 1. How Doth the Little Crocodile 1
Lesson 2. The Walrus and The Carpenter 6
Lesson 3. Christmas Greetings 12
Lesson 4. Beautiful Soup 15

POET II: JAMES WHITCOMB RILEY
Lesson 5. A Life Lesson 18
Lesson 6. The Raggedy Man 22
Lesson 7. Little Orphant Annie 26
Lesson 8. When the Frost is on the Punkin 31

POET III: MARY AUSTIN
Lesson 9. Hunting Weather 35
Lesson 10. Signs of Spring 39
Lesson 11. The Sandhill Crane 42
Lesson 12. Blue-Eyed Grass 45
Lesson 13. Prairie-Dog Town 48

POET IV: EUGENE FIELD
Lesson 14. Wynken, Blynken, and Nod 51
Lesson 15. Little Blue Pigeon 57
Lesson 16. The Sugar Plum Tree 60
Lesson 17. The Duel 63
Lesson 18. Jest 'Fore Christmas 66

POET V: ROBERT LOUIS STEVENSON
Lesson 19. Fifteen Men on the Dead Man's Chest 71
Lesson 20. A Good Boy 76
Lesson 21. Windy Nights 79
Lesson 22. The Swing 81
Lesson 23. My Shadow 84

POET VI: ELLA WHEELER WILCOX
Lesson 24. Solitude 87
Lesson 25. A Fable 92
Lesson 26. Sunset 96
Lesson 27. A March Snow 99

POET VII: ABBIE FARWELL BROWN
Lesson 28. The Fisherman 102
Lesson 29. Friends 106
Lesson 30. The Faithless Flowers 109
Lesson 31. Baby's Valentine 112
Lesson 32. A Tryst 116

POET VIII: SARA TEASDALE
Lesson 33. There Will Come Soft Rains 119
Lesson 34. Barter 123
Lesson 35. Let It Be Forgotten 126
Lesson 36. Wishes 129

ANSWERS TO REVIEW QUESTIONS 132

REFERENCES 140

Goals of This Book Series

This book series aims to familiarize children with works of poetry from an early age, nurture the imagination, inspire an appreciation for beauty, encourage a mind for symbolism and nuance, foster the ability to narrate complex ideas, and expand children's vocabularies and geographical knowledge. Lessons are short and interactive by design to target elementary school-aged children.

Inspiration for This Book Series

Charlotte Mason, born in 1842, sought to provide teaching advice and strategies to instructors and homeschooling parents. She detailed her educational philosophies and methodologies in her multi-volume *Home Education Series*. She advocated for centering instruction around living works, such as the finest art, music, poetry, and prose. Mason recommended that from an early age, children engage in the regular study of poetry, including reciting poetry. In her *Home Education Series*, she writes, "…include a good deal of poetry, to accustom him to the delicate rendering of shades of meaning, and especially to make him aware that words are beautiful in themselves, that they are a source of pleasure, and are worthy of our honour; and that a beautiful word deserves to be beautifully said, with a certain roundness of tone and precision of utterance."

The Targeted Audience for This Book

This book targets elementary school-aged children in grades one and up.

Overview of This Book

This book provides 36 lessons, or enough for one lesson per week over a standard 36-week school year. This volume highlights eight master poets and their poetry. Children study four to five poems by each poet with one new poem introduced weekly. The selected poems in this book appeal to children and their adult instructors by featuring nature, animals, love, friendship, the seasons, holidays, trials, and triumphs.

This volume features the following poets:
- Lewis Carroll
- James Whitcomb Riley
- Mary Austin
- Eugene Field
- Robert Louis Stevenson
- Ella Wheeler Wilcox
- Abbie Farwell Brown
- Sara Teasdale

How to Teach Using This Book

The tables below outline the recommended instructional approach to teach a 36-week course using this book.

Every Four to Five Weeks – Introduce a New Poet	
Section Title	**Section Instructions**
Poet Overview	Instructors and students read and discuss the biographical information of the poet.
Color the Poet	Students color the portrait of the poet.
Map the Poet	Students find and color geographical locations related to the poet.

Every Week – Introduce a New Poem	
Section Title	**Section Instructions**
Featured Poem	• Instructors read the poem aloud to students. • Students practice reciting the poem with instructor assistance. • Students color poem illustrations as desired.
Synopsis	Instructors and students review the synopsis of the poem.
Recite Poem Information	Students practice reciting the poem title and the name of the poet.
Narrate the Poem	Students verbally summarize the poem in their own words.
Study Poem Pictures	Students describe how the included pictures relate to the poem.
Can You Find It?	Students find and point out items in poem pictures.
Vocabulary	• Students practice pronouncing the featured vocabulary words. • Students copy the vocabulary words. • Students recite vocabulary word definitions with instructor assistance.
Review Questions	• Instructors ask students the review questions. • Answers to review questions are included at the end of the book.
Coloring and Copywork	• Students color artwork related to the poem. • Students trace and/or copy the provided poem excerpt.

POET I: LEWIS CARROLL
LESSON 1. "HOW DOTH THE LITTLE CROCODILE"

POET OVERVIEW

- Charles Lutwidge Dodgson (Lewis Carroll) was born in 1832 in Guildford, England.
- The son of a country parson, Carroll had ten brothers and sisters.
- As a young child, Carroll became ill, resulting in deafness in one ear. Carroll also suffered from a stammer.
- Carroll was homeschooled until he was twelve, at which time he went away to school. He went on to study mathematics at Oxford.
- From when he was a child, Carroll wrote short stories and poetry and submitted them to magazines.
- Carroll is most famous for writing "Alice's Adventures in Wonderland."
- Carroll died of pneumonia in Guildford, England at the age of 65.

COLOR THE POET

MAP THE POET

Locate and color Carroll's country of birth, **England (Southern United Kingdom)**, on the map of Europe.

FEATURED POEM (Children Practice Reciting the Poem with Instructor Assistance.)

How doth the little crocodile
Improve his shining tail,
And pour the waters of the Nile
On every golden scale!

How cheerfully he seems to grin
How neatly spreads his claws,
And welcomes little fishes in,
With gently smiling jaws!

SYNOPSIS

A crocodile bathes in the Nile River and eats little fishes.

ENRICHMENT ACTIVITIES

1. **Recite Poem Information**
   Recite the title of the poem and the name of the poet.
2. **Narrate the Poem**
   Narrate the poem events aloud using your own words.
3. **Study the Poem Picture**
   Study the poem picture and describe how it relates to the poem.
4. **Can You Find It?**
   Find the following in the poem picture: sharp teeth, jaws, claws, scales, eyes, snout, and nostril.
5. **Act Out the Poem**
   - Pretend to be the crocodile hunting in the Nile River.
   - Swim through the warm waters of the river.
   - Smile with your mouth and spread out your claws to scoop up little fishes.

6. **Map the Poem**
    - In the poem, the crocodile hunts for fishes in the waters of the Nile River.
    - Study the map of Egypt to find the Nile River. Color Egypt yellow with a crayon or colored pencil.
    - The Nile flows north. Trace the northern flow of the Nile River in blue.
    - Into which sea does the Nile flow? Color the sea purple.

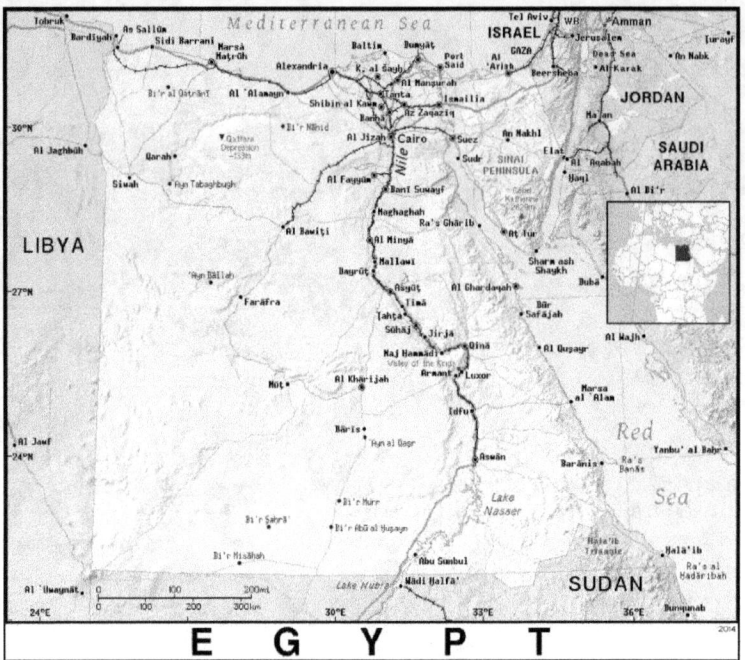

VOCABULARY

Recite and Copy Each Word	Recite the Definition
Nile *Nile*	A large river in Africa flowing into the Mediterranean Sea.
scale	Hard overlapping plate covering the skin of reptiles or fishes.
jaws	The bones, usually bearing teeth, which form the framework of the mouth.

REVIEW QUESTIONS

1. What is the title of the poem?
2. What is the name of the poet who wrote "The Crocodile?"
3. What happens in the poem?
4. Where does the poem take place?
5. List the animal characters in the poem.

ELEMENTARY POETRY VOLUME 3: POETRY OF NATURE, REVELRY, AND RHYME

COLORING AND COPYWORK

How doth the little crocodile

improve his shining tail.

LESSON 2. "THE WALRUS AND THE CARPENTER" BY LEWIS CARROLL

FEATURED POEM

The sun was shining on the sea,
Shining with all his might:
He did his very best to make
The billows smooth and bright--
And this was odd, because it was
The middle of the night.

The moon was shining sulkily,
Because she thought the sun
Had got no business to be there
After the day was done--
"It's very rude of him," she said,
"To come and spoil the fun!"

The sea was wet as wet could be,
The sands were dry as dry.
You could not see a cloud, because
No cloud was in the sky:
No birds were flying overhead--
There were no birds to fly.

The Walrus and the Carpenter
Were walking close at hand;
They wept like anything to see
Such quantities of sand:
"If this were only cleared away,"
They said, "it would be grand!"

"If seven maids with seven mops
Swept it for half a year.
Do you suppose," the Walrus said,
"That they could get it clear?"
"I doubt it," said the Carpenter,
And shed a bitter tear.

"O Oysters, come and walk with us!"
The Walrus did beseech.
"A pleasant walk, a pleasant talk,
Along the briny beach:
We cannot do with more than four,
To give a hand to each."

The eldest Oyster looked at him,
But never a word he said:
The eldest Oyster winked his eye,
And shook his heavy head--
Meaning to say he did not choose
To leave the oyster-bed.

But four young Oysters hurried up,
All eager for the treat:
Their coats were brushed, their faces washed,
Their shoes were clean and neat--
And this was odd, because, you know,
They hadn't any feet.

Four other Oysters followed them,
And yet another four;
And thick and fast they came at last,
And more, and more, and more--
All hopping through the frothy waves,
And scrambling to the shore.

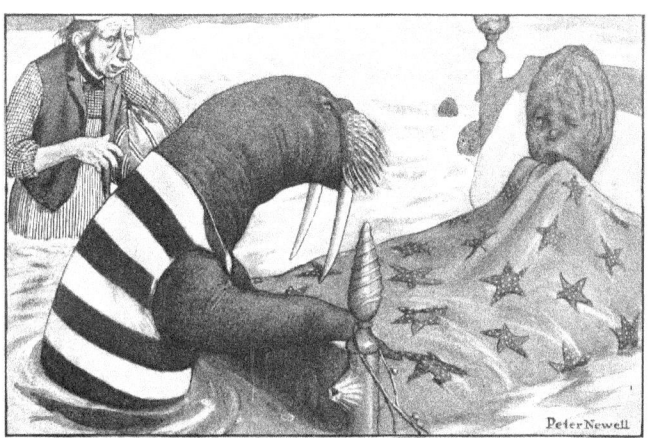

The Walrus and the Carpenter
Walked on a mile or so,
And then they rested on a rock
Conveniently low:
And all the little Oysters stood
And waited in a row.

"The time has come," the Walrus said,
"To talk of many things:
Of shoes--and ships--and sealing-wax--
Of cabbages--and kings--
And why the sea is boiling hot--
And whether pigs have wings."

"But wait a bit," the Oysters cried,
"Before we have our chat;
For some of us are out of breath,
And all of us are fat!"
"No hurry!" said the Carpenter.
They thanked him much for that.

"A loaf of bread," the Walrus said,
"Is what we chiefly need:
Pepper and vinegar besides
Are very good indeed--
Now if you're ready, Oysters dear,
We can begin to feed."

"But not on us!" the Oysters cried,
Turning a little blue.
"After such kindness, that would be
A dismal thing to do!"
"The night is fine," the Walrus said.
"Do you admire the view?

"It was so kind of you to come!
And you are very nice!"
The Carpenter said nothing but
"Cut us another slice:
I wish you were not quite so deaf--
I've had to ask you twice!"

"It seems a shame," the Walrus said,
"To play them such a trick,
After we've brought them out so far,
And made them trot so quick!"
The Carpenter said nothing but
"The butter's spread too thick!"

"I weep for you," the Walrus said:
"I deeply sympathize."
With sobs and tears he sorted out
Those of the largest size,
Holding his pocket-handkerchief
Before his streaming eyes.

"O Oysters," said the Carpenter,
"You've had a pleasant run!
Shall we be trotting home again?"
But answer came there none--
And this was scarcely odd, because
They'd eaten every one.

SYNOPSIS

The sun shines in the middle of the night as the Walrus and the Carpenter walk along the beach and discuss how to remove all the sand. The Walrus and the Carpenter invite the Oysters to walk with them. The eldest Oyster refuses, but many other Oysters agree. The Walrus, the Carpenter, and the Oysters walk on the beach. When the Walrus mentions needing pepper and vinegar, condiments used to season oysters, the oysters worry they are about to be eaten. At the end of the poem, the Carpenter asks the Oysters if they wish to return home, but no Oysters answer. The Walrus and Carpenter have eaten them all.

ENRICHMENT ACTIVITIES

1. **Recite Poem Information**
   Recite the title of the poem and the name of the poet.
2. **Narrate the Poem**
   Narrate the poem events aloud using your own words.
3. **Study the Poem Pictures**
   Study the poem pictures and describe how they relate to the poem.
4. **Can You Find It?**
   Find the following in the poem pictures:
   - Picture #1: Walrus, Carpenter, tears, sea, billows, and hand drill.
   - Picture #2: tusks, eldest oyster, "oyster bed," and stars.
   - Picture #3: bread, empty oyster shells, and pocket-handkerchief.
5. **Identify Oddities in the Poem**
   - Identify any oddities or strange happenings in the poem.
   - For example, the sun shining at night.

VOCABULARY

Recite and Copy Each Word	Recite the Definition
billows	Large waves.
sulkily	In a moping, sullen, or ill-tempered manner.
walrus	A large Arctic marine mammal with tusks, wrinkled skin, and four flippers.
carpenter	A person skilled at cutting and joining timber to construct buildings.

Recite and Copy Each Word	Recite the Definition
oyster	A sea animal of soft flesh protected by a hinged shell.
frothy	Foamy; churned to the point of containing bubbles.
vinegar	A sour condiment used to season oysters.
dismal	Gloomy, bleak, or depressing.
trot	A gait of a person faster than a walk but slower than a run.
sympathize	To show a feeling of pity for the suffering of another.
odd	Strange or peculiar.

REVIEW QUESTIONS

1. What is the title of the poem?
2. What is the name of the poet who wrote "The Walrus and The Carpenter?"
3. What happens in the poem?
4. Where does the poem take place?
5. Who are the characters in the poem?
6. Why is the moon mad at the sun?
7. Why do the oysters worry about being eaten when the Walrus mentions pepper and vinegar?
8. What does the poem teach the reader?

ELEMENTARY POETRY VOLUME 3: POETRY OF NATURE, REVELRY, AND RHYME

COLORING AND COPYWORK

But answer come there none—

And this was scarcely odd,

They'd eaten every one.

LESSON 3. "CHRISTMAS GREETINGS (FROM A FAIRY TO A CHILD)" BY LEWIS CARROLL

FEATURED POEM

Lady dear, if Fairies may
For a moment lay aside
Cunning tricks and elfish play,
'Tis at happy Christmas-tide.

We have heard the children say -
Gentle children, whom we love -
Long ago, on Christmas Day,
Came a message from above.

Still, as Christmastide comes round,
They remember it again -
Echo still the joyful sound
"Peace on earth, goodwill to men!"

Yet the hearts must childlike be
Where such heavenly guests abide:
Unto children, in their glee,
All the year is Christmas-tide!

Thus, forgetting tricks and play
For a moment, Lady dear,
We would wish you, if we may,
Merry Christmas, glad New Year!

SYNOPSIS

The fairy narrator puts trickery aside to wish a child a merry Christmas and a glad New Year.

ENRICHMENT ACTIVITIES

1. **Recite Poem Information**
   Recite the title of the poem and the name of the poet.

2. **Narrate the Poem**
   Narrate the poem events aloud using your own words.

3. **Study the Poem Picture**
   Study the poem picture and describe how it relates to the poem.

4. **Can You Find It?**
   Find the following in the poem picture: ornaments, doll, soldier, horse, saddle, trunk, candles, tree topper, tree stand, house, train, garland, and ball.

VOCABULARY

Recite and Copy Each Word	Recite the Definition
cunning	Sly, crafty, artful, or skillful.
echo	An utterance repeating what has just been said.
glee	Joy or happiness.

REVIEW QUESTIONS

1. What is the title of the poem?
2. What is the name of the poet who wrote "Christmas Greetings?"
3. What happens in the poem?
4. Who are the characters in the poem?
5. What does the poem teach the reader?

COLORING AND COPYWORK

Echo still the joyful sound

Peace on earth, goodwill to men

LESSON 4. "BEAUTIFUL SOUP"
BY LEWIS CARROLL

FEATURED POEM

Beautiful Soup, so rich and green,
Waiting in a hot tureen!
Who for such dainties would not stoop?
Soup of the evening, beautiful Soup!
Soup of the evening, beautiful Soup!

Beau-ootiful Soo-oop!
Beau-ootiful Soo-oop!
Soo-oop of the e-e-evening,
Beautiful, beautiful Soup!

Beautiful Soup! Who cares for fish,
Game, or any other dish?
Who would not give all else for two
Pennyworth only of Beautiful Soup?
Pennyworth only of beautiful Soup?

Beau-ootiful Soo-oop!
Beau-ootiful Soo-oop!
Soo-oop of the e-e-evening,
Beautiful, beauti-FUL SOUP!

SYNOPSIS

The narrator describes his love of beautiful, green soup served in a hot tureen.

ENRICHMENT ACTIVITIES

1. **Recite Poem Information**
   Recite the title of the poem and the name of the poet.

2. **Narrate the Poem**
   Narrate the poem events aloud using your own words.

3. **Study the Poem Picture**
   Study the poem picture and describe how it relates to the poem.

4. **Can You Find It?**
   Find the following in the poem picture: soup, tureen, and utensil handle.

5. **Discuss Soup**
   - Do you love soup as much as Lewis Carroll?
   - Which types of soup have you tried?
   - What is your favorite kind of soup?
   - Which ingredients have you eaten in soups? List the spices, vegetables, meats, legumes, and pasta shapes.
6. **Act Out the Poem**
   Serve some soup (real or pretend) and recite the poem to your bowl of soup.

VOCABULARY

Recite and Copy Each Word	Recite the Definition
tureen	A deep covered dish from which soup is served.
dainties	Something good to eat or a delicacy.
stoop	Bend one's head or body forward and downward.
game	Wild mammals or birds hunted for sport or food.
pennyworth	An amount of something that may be bought for a penny.

REVIEW QUESTIONS

1. What is the title of the poem?
2. What is the name of the poet who wrote "Beautiful Soup?"
3. What happens in the poem?
4. Where does the poem take place?
5. Who are the characters in the poem?
6. What does the poem teach the reader?

COLORING AND COPYWORK

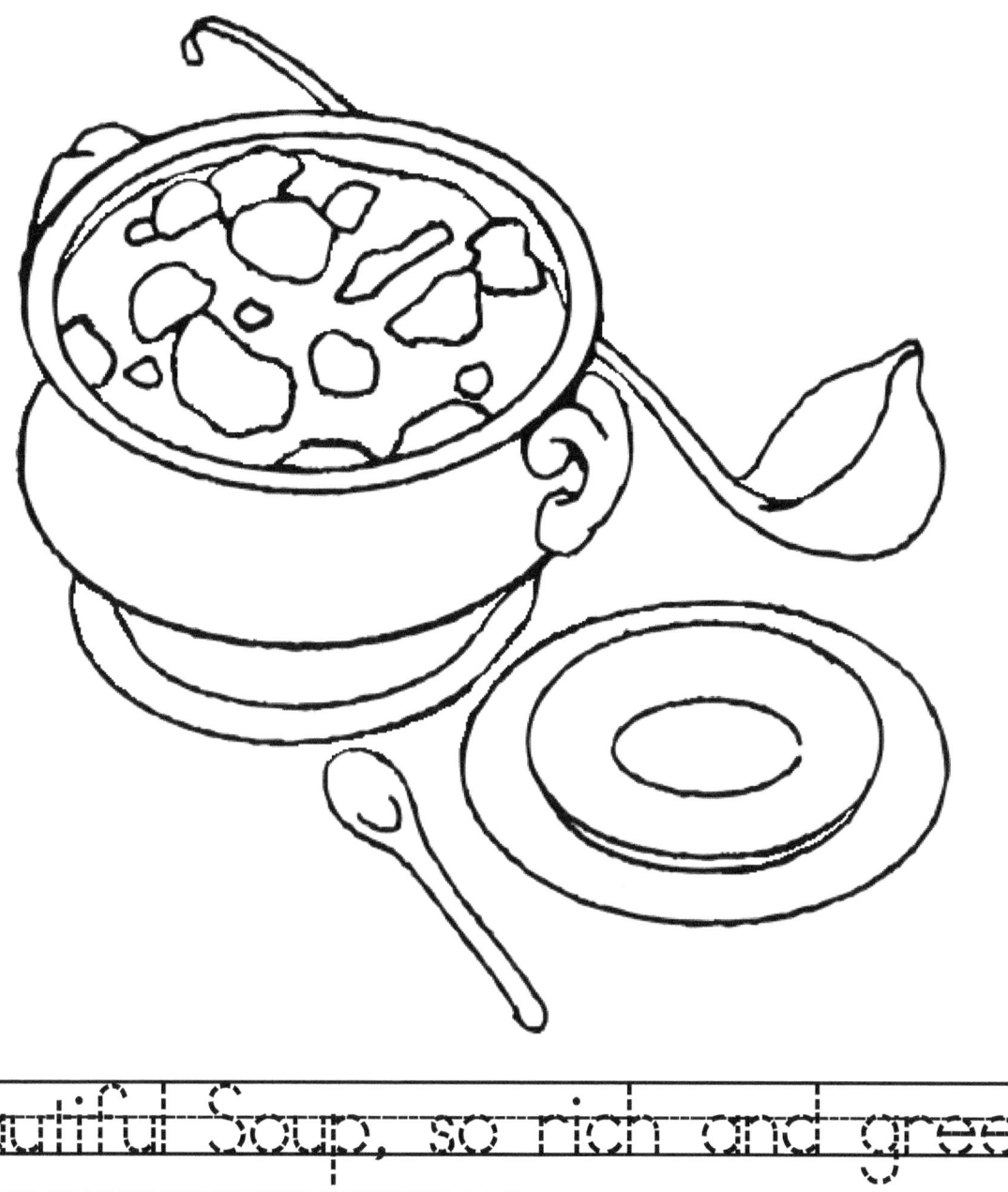

Beautiful Soup, so rich and green

Waiting in a hot tureen

SONJA GLUMICH

POET II: JAMES WHITCOMB RILEY
LESSON 5. "A LIFE LESSON"

POET OVERVIEW

- James Whitcomb Riley was born in 1849 in Greenfield, Indiana.
- Riley had five siblings. His mother taught him to read at home before sending him to school.
- From when he was a child, Carroll wrote short stories and poetry and submitted them to magazines.
- Riley frequently encountered trouble at school and disliked his teachers, which he later wrote about in his poems.
- Riley wrote approximately 1000 poems during his lifetime and became famous by going on poetry tours across America.
- Riley was known as the "Hoosier poet." A "Hoosier" is a native or inhabitant of Indiana. Some of Riley's poems were written in a Hoosier dialect, including "The Raggedy Man," "Little Orphant Annie," and "When the Frost is on the Punkin."
- Riley suffered from alcoholism and never married or had children. Riley died in 1916 at the age of 66 in Indianapolis, Indiana.

COLOR THE POET

MAP THE POET

Locate and color Riley's state of birth, **Indiana (IN)**, on the map of the United States.

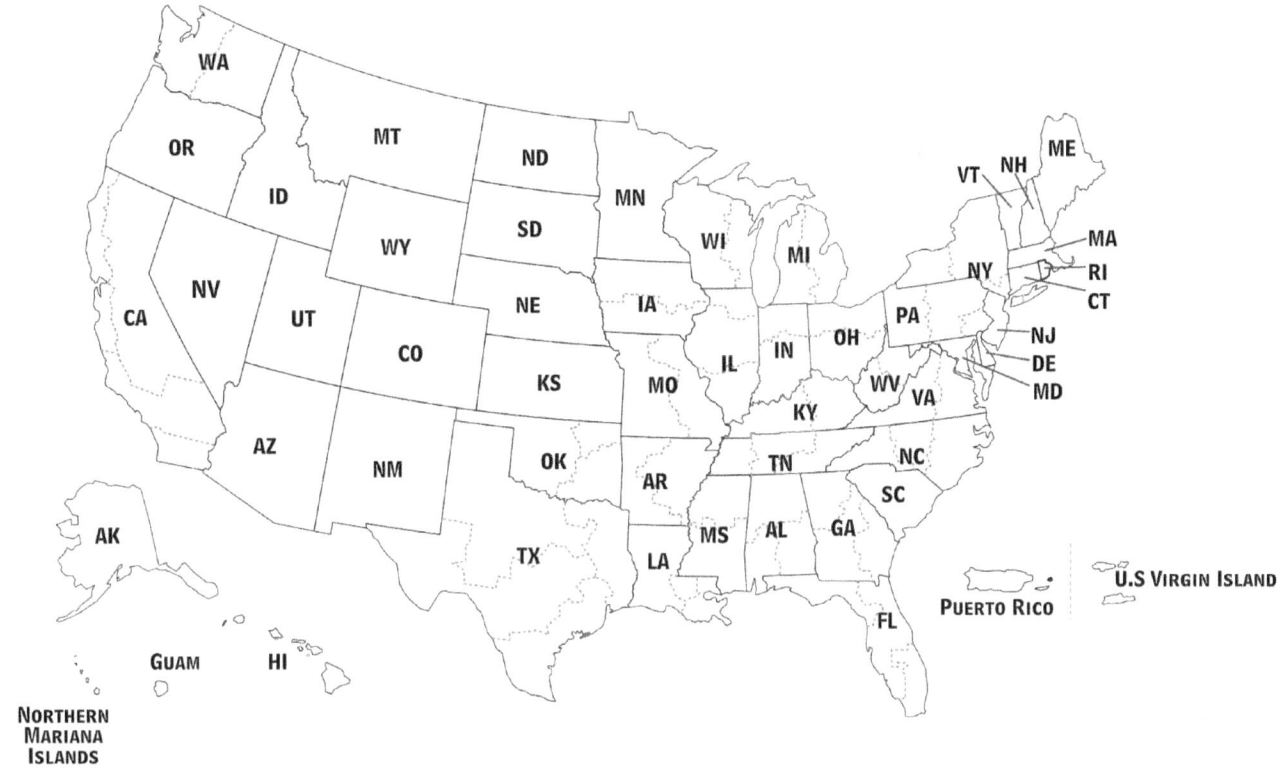

FEATURED POEM (Children Practice Reciting the Poem with Instructor Assistance.)

1. There! little girl; don't cry!
They have broken your doll, I know;
And your tea-set blue,
And your play-house, too,
Are things of the long ago;
But childish troubles will soon pass by. --
There! little girl; don't cry!

2. There! little girl; don't cry!
They have broken your slate, I know;
And the glad, wild ways
Of your schoolgirl days
Are things of the long ago;
But life and love will soon come by. --
There! little girl; don't cry!

3. There! little girl; don't cry!
They have broken your heart I know;
And the rainbow gleams
Of your youthful dreams
Are things of the long ago;
But Heaven holds all for which you sigh.
There! little girl; don't cry!

SYNOPSIS

The poem moves through the difficulties faced by a girl as she grows up. The narrator reminds the girl that her troubles are temporary and that better days are ahead.

ENRICHMENT ACTIVITIES

1. **Recite Poem Information**
   Recite the title of the poem and the name of the poet.
2. **Narrate the Poem**
   Narrate the poem events aloud using your own words.
3. **Study the Poem Picture**
   Study the poem picture and describe how it relates to the poem.
4. **Can You Find It?**
   Find the following in the poem picture: little girl, lady, someone crying, and someone comforting.
5. **Discuss Difficulties**
   - Discuss a difficulty you faced in your past.
   - Did you cry because of the difficulty?
   - Discuss who you can turn to for help in times of difficulty.
   - Do you agree that in times of trouble, better days are ahead of us?

VOCABULARY

Recite and Copy Each Word	Recite the Definition
slate	A sheet of slate rock for writing on with chalk or with a thin rod of slate (a slate pencil) formerly commonly used by younger children for writing practice in schools.
gleams	Shines, glitters, or glistens.
youthful	Young or seeming young.

REVIEW QUESTIONS

1. What is the title of the poem?
2. What is the name of the poet who wrote "A Life Lesson?"
3. What happens in the poem?
4. Who are the characters in the poem?
5. What does the poem teach the reader?

COLORING AND COPYWORK

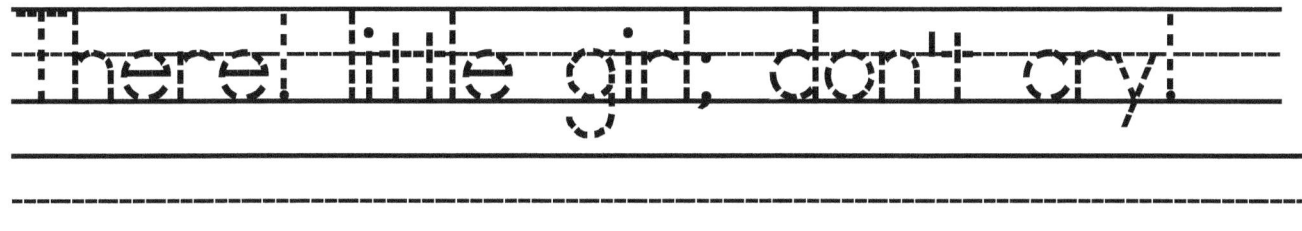

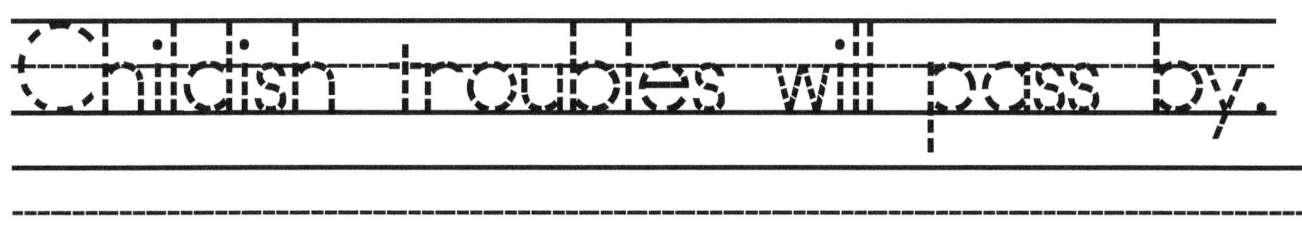

LESSON 6. "THE RAGGEDY MAN" BY JAMES WHITCOMB RILEY

FEATURED POEM

1. O the Raggedy Man! He works fer Pa;
An' he's the goodest man ever you saw!
He comes to our house every day,
An' waters the horses, an' feeds 'em hay;
An' he opens the shed—an' we all ist laugh
When he drives out our little old wobble-ly calf;
An' nen—ef our hired girl says he can—
He milks the cow fer 'Lizabuth Ann.—
Ain't he a' awful good Raggedy Man?
Raggedy! Raggedy! Raggedy Man!

2. W'y, The Raggedy Man—he's ist so good,
He splits the kindlin' an' chops the wood;
An' nen he spades in our garden, too,
An' does most things 'at boys can't do.—
He clumbed clean up in our big tree
An' shooked a' apple down fer me—
An' 'nother 'n', too, fer 'Lizabuth Ann—
An' 'nother 'n', too, fer The Raggedy Man.—
Ain't he a' awful kind Raggedy Man?
Raggedy! Raggedy! Raggedy Man!

3. An' The Raggedy Man one time say he
Pick' roast' rambos from a' orchurd-tree,
An' et 'em—all ist roast' an' hot!—
An' it's so, too!—'cause a corn-crib got
Afire one time an' all burn' down
On "The Smoot Farm," 'bout four mile from town—
On "The Smoot Farm"! Yes—an' the hired han'
'At worked there nen 'uz The Raggedy Man!—
Ain't he the beatin'est Raggedy Man?
Raggedy! Raggedy! Raggedy Man!

4. The Raggedy Man's so good an' kind
He'll be our "horsey," an' "haw" an' mind
Ever'thing 'at you make him do—
An' won't run off—'less you want him to!
I drived him wunst way down our lane
An' he got skeered, when it 'menced to rain,
An' ist rared up an' squealed and run
Purt' nigh away!—an' it's all in fun!
Nen he skeered ag'in at a' old tin can ...
Whoa! y' old runaway Raggedy Man!
Raggedy! Raggedy! Raggedy Man!

5. An' The Raggedy Man, he knows most rhymes,
An' tells 'em, ef I be good, sometimes:
Knows 'bout Giunts, an' Griffuns, an' Elves,
An' the Squidgicum-Squees 'at swallers the'rselves:
An', wite by the pump in our pasture-lot,
He showed me the hole 'at the Wunks is got,
'At lives 'way deep in the ground, an' can
Turn into me, er 'Lizabuth Ann!
Er Ma, er Pa, er The Raggedy Man!
Ain't he a funny old Raggedy Man?
Raggedy! Raggedy! Raggedy Man!

6. An' wunst, when The Raggedy Man come late,
An' pigs ist root' thue the garden-gate,
He 'tend like the pigs 'uz bears an' said,
"Old Bear-shooter'll shoot 'em dead!"
An' race' an' chase' 'em, an' they'd ist run
When he pint his hoe at 'em like it's a gun
An' go "Bang!—Bang!" nen 'tend he stan'
An' load up his gun ag'in! Raggedy Man!
He's an old Bear-shooter Raggedy Man!
Raggedy! Raggedy! Raggedy Man!

7. An' sometimes The Raggedy Man lets on
We're little prince-children, an' old King's gone
To git more money, an' lef' us there—
And Robbers is ist thick ever'where;
An' nen—ef we all won't cry, fer shore—
The Raggedy Man he'll come and "splore
The Castul-halls," an' steal the "gold"—
An' steal us, too, an' grab an' hold
An' pack us off to his old "Cave"!—An'
Haymow's the "cave" o' The Raggedy Man!—
Raggedy! Raggedy! Raggedy Man!

8. The Raggedy Man—one time, when he
Wuz makin' a little bow-'n'-orry fer me,
Says "When you're big like your Pa is,
Air you go' to keep a fine store like his—
An' be a rich merchunt—an' wear fine clothes?—
Er what air you go' to be, goodness knows?"
An' nen he laughed at 'Lizabuth Ann,
An' I says "'M go' to be a Raggedy Man!—
I'm ist go' to be a nice Raggedy Man!"
Raggedy! Raggedy! Raggedy Man!

SYNOPSIS

The poem describes a farm worker that the boyish narrator calls *The Raggedy Man*. In the second half of the poem, Raggedy Man tells rhymes and tales of giants, pretends pigs are bears and his hoe is a bear-shooter, and plays games of kings and robbers. The Raggedy Man asks the narrator if he will be a rich merchant like his father. Instead, the narrator aspires to be a nice Raggedy Man. The Raggedy Man is based on a real person, a German worker hired by James Whitcomb Riley's father.

ENRICHMENT ACTIVITIES

1. **Recite Poem Information**
   Recite the title of the poem and the name of the poet.

2. **Narrate the Poem**
   Narrate the poem events aloud using your own words.

3. **Study the Poem Pictures**
   Study the poem pictures and describe how they relate to the poem.

4. **Can You Find It?**
   Find the following in the poem pictures: Raggedy Man, narrator, suspenders, hat, horse, barn, and farm tools (rake, sickle).

VOCABULARY

Recite and Copy Each Word	Recite the Definition
wite	Right.
wunks	Shapeshifting creatures.
wunst (once)	On one occasion or for one time only.
'tend	Pretend.
'uz	Was.
castul	Castle.
haymow	A stack of hay.
bow-'n'-orry	Bow and arrow.
air	Are.

REVIEW QUESTIONS

1. What is the title of the poem?
2. What is the name of the poet who wrote "The Raggedy Man?"
3. What happens in the poem?
4. Where does the poem take place?
5. Who are the characters in the poem?
6. What does the poem teach the reader?

COLORING AND COPYWORK

Raggedy Man! He works fer Pa,

The goodest man ever you saw!

LESSON 7. "LITTLE ORPHANT ANNIE" BY JAMES WHITCOMB RILEY

FEATURED POEM

To all the little children: -- The happy ones; and sad ones;
The sober and the silent ones; the boisterous and glad ones;
The good ones -- Yes, the good ones, too; and all the lovely bad ones.

Little Orphant Annie's come to our house to stay,
An' wash the cups an' saucers up, an' brush the crumbs away,
An' shoo the chickens off the porch, an' dust the hearth, an' sweep,
An' make the fire, an' bake the bread, an' earn her board-an'-keep;
An' all us other childern, when the supper-things is done,
We set around the kitchen fire an' has the mostest fun
A-list'nin' to the witch-tales 'at Annie tells about,
An' the Gobble-uns 'at gits you
Ef You Don't Watch Out!

Wunst they wuz a little boy wouldn't say his prayers,--
An' when he went to bed at night, away up-stairs,
His Mammy heerd him holler, an' his Daddy heerd him bawl,
An' when they turn't the kivvers down, he wuzn't there at all!
An' they seeked him in the rafter-room, an' cubby-hole, an' press,
An' seeked him up the chimbly-flue, an' ever'-wheres, I guess;
But all they ever found wuz thist his pants an' roundabout:--
An' the Gobble-uns 'll git you
Ef You Don't Watch Out!

An' one time a little girl 'ud allus laugh an' grin,
An' make fun of ever' one, an' all her blood-an'-kin;
An' wunst, when they was 'company,' an' ole folks wuz there,
She mocked 'em an' shocked 'em, an' said she didn't care!
An' thist as she kicked her heels, an' turn't to run an' hide,
They wuz two great big Black Things a-standin' by her side,
An' they snatched her through the ceilin' 'fore she knowed what she's about!
An' the Gobble-uns 'll git you
Ef You Don't Watch Out!

An' little Orphant Annie says, when the blaze is blue,
An' the lamp-wick sputters, an' the wind goes woo-oo!
An' you hear the crickets quit, an' the moon is gray,
An' the lightnin'-bugs in dew is all squenched away,--
You better mind yer parunts, an' yer teachurs fond an' dear,
An' churish them 'at
loves you, an' dry the orphant's tear,
An' he'p the pore an' needy ones 'at clusters all about,
Er the Gobble-uns 'll git you
Ef You Don't Watch Out!

SYNOPSIS

An orphan named Annie comes to live with the young narrators of the poem. Annie gathers the children around the fire and tells spooky tales of goblins getting disobedient and greedy children.

ENRICHMENT ACTIVITIES

1. **Recite Poem Information**
   Recite the title of the poem and the name of the poet.

2. **Narrate the Poem**
   Narrate the poem events aloud using your own words.

3. **Study the Poem Picture**
   Study the poem picture and describe how it relates to the poem.

4. **Can You Find It?**
   Find the following in the poem picture: Little Orphant Annie, narrators, kettle, hearth, candlesticks, shadows, smoke, suspenders, and chair.

5. **Learn the History of the Poem**
   - James Whitcomb Riley based the poem on an orphan named Mary Alice "Allie" Smith who lived with his family. Study the photograph of the real Allie, taken long ago in 1863.
   - Riley originally titled the poem, "Little Orphant Allie," but a mistake during printing changed the poem title to "Little Orphant Annie."
   - The "Little Orphan Annie" comic strip and the Raggedy Ann doll are named after "Little Orphant Annie."

VOCABULARY

Recite and Copy Each Word	Recite the Definition
orphant	Orphan.
hearth	The floor of a fireplace.
board	Regular meals or the amount paid for them in a place of lodging.
keep	The food or money required to keep someone alive and healthy.
gobble-uns	Goblins.
wunst	Once.
wuz / wuzn't	Was / Wasn't.
kivvers	Covers.
rafter-room	Attic.

Recite and Copy Each Word	Recite the Definition
cubby-hole	A small, snug room which may be used as a place of privacy and safety by children.
'ud	Who'd.
allus	Always.
ever' one	Everyone.
mocked	Taunted or made fun of by mimicking.
lamp-wick	A bundle, twist, braid, or woven strip of cord, fabric, fiber, or other porous material in a candle, oil lamp, kerosene heater, or the like.
sputters	Throws out something, as little jets of steam, with a noise like that made by one sputtering.
squenched	Put out or extinguished.
churish	Cherish.
pore (poor)	With little or no possessions or money.

REVIEW QUESTIONS

1. What is the title of the poem?
2. What is the name of the poet who wrote "Little Orphant Annie?"
3. What happens in the poem?
4. Where does the poem take place?
5. Who are the characters in the poem?
6. What does the poem teach the reader?

COLORING AND COPYWORK

An' the Gobble-uns 'at gits you

Ef You Don't Watch Out!

LESSON 8. "WHEN THE FROST IS ON THE PUNKIN" BY JAMES WHITCOMB RILEY

FEATURED POEM

When the frost is on the punkin and the fodder's in the shock
And you hear the kyouck and gobble of the struttin' turkey cock
And the clackin' of the guineys, and the cluckin' of the hens
And the rooster's hallylooyer as he tiptoes on the fence
O, it's then's the times a feller is a-feelin' at his best
With the risin' sun to greet him from a night of peaceful rest
As he leaves the house, bareheaded, and goes out to feed the stock
When the frost is on the punkin and the fodder's in the shock

They's something kindo' harty-like about the atmusfere
When the heat of summer's over and the coolin' fall is here
Of course we miss the flowers, and the blossums on the trees
And the mumble of the hummin'-birds and buzzin' of the bees
But the air's so appetizin'; and the landscape through the haze
Of a crisp and sunny morning of the airly autumn days
Is a pictur' that no painter has the colorin' to mock
When the frost is on the punkin and the fodder's in the shock.

The husky, rusty russel of the tossels of the corn,
And the raspin' of the tangled leaves, as golden as the morn;
The stubble in the furries kindo' lonesome-like, but still
A-preachin' sermuns to us of the barns they growed to fill;
The strawstack in the medder, and the reaper in the shed;
The hosses in theyr stalls below the clover over-head!
O, it sets my hart a-clickin' like the tickin' of a clock,
When the frost is on the punkin and the fodder's in the shock!

Then your apples all is gethered, and the ones a feller keeps
Is poured around the celler-floor in red and yeller heaps;
And your cider-makin' 's over, and your wimmern-folks is through
With their mince and apple butter, and theyr souse and saussage, too!
I don't know how to tell it but ef sich a thing could be
As the Angels wantin' boardin', and they'd call around on me
I'd want to 'commodate 'em all the whole-indurin' flock
When the frost is on the punkin and the fodder's in the shock!

SYNOPSIS

The poem praises the sights, sounds, sensations, and foods of farm life during the autumn season.

ENRICHMENT ACTIVITIES

1. **Recite Poem Information**
   Recite the title of the poem and the name of the poet.
2. **Narrate the Poem**
   Narrate the poem events aloud using your own words.
3. **Study the Poem Picture**
   Study the poem picture and describe how it relates to the poem.
4. **Can You Find It?**
   Find the following in the poem picture: tail feathers, feet, beak, wattle, and wings.
5. **Take a Morning Walk, and Write a Poem**
   - One morning this week, read the poem for inspiration and then take a walk.
   - Take special note of the sights and sounds of nature during your stroll.
   - Create a poem based on anything beautiful or inspiring that you see on your walk.

VOCABULARY

Recite and Copy Each Word	Recite the Definition
punkin	Pumpkin.
fodder	Food for animals.
shock	An arrangement of stalks and ears of corn bound together for drying, a stook.
struttin' (strutting)	1. To stand or walk stiffly, with the tail erect and spread out. 2. To walk proudly or haughtily.
guineys (guinea fowls)	Any of several birds resembling partridges.
stock	Grain such as corn or wheat stacked in upright piles for drying.

Recite and Copy Each Word	Recite the Definition
atmusfere (atmosphere)	1. The air in a particular place. 2. The apparent mood felt in an environment.
airly	Early.
tossels (corn tassels)	The loose strands or threads on a male plant of corn or maize.
medder (meadow)	A field or pasture, especially one covered with grass to be mown for hay.
reaper	A person, tool, or machine that harvests crops.
wimmern	Women.
mince (mincemeat)	A mixture of fruit, spices and sugar used as a filling for mince pies.
'commodate	Accommodate.

REVIEW QUESTIONS

1. What is the title of the poem?
2. What is the name of the poet who wrote "When the Frost is on the Punkin?"
3. What happens in the poem?
4. Where does the poem take place?
5. Who are the characters in the poem?
6. What does the poem teach the reader?

COLORING AND COPYWORK

When the frost is on the punkin

and the fodder's in the shock.

POET III: MARY AUSTIN
LESSON 9. "HUNTING WEATHER"

POET OVERVIEW

- Mary Austin was born in 1868 in Carlinville, Illinois.
- Austin grew up in a large family with six siblings.
- After Austin graduated from college, her family moved to California to establish a homestead. The United States Homestead Act of 1862 offered 160 acres of land to any citizens willing to live on and farm the land for five years.
- Austin wrote poems, plays, and novels over her lifetime. She also helped to establish two theaters.
- Austin's poetry often featured the plants, animals, and people of the American Southwest.
- Austin had a mountain named after her. Mount Mary Austin is in California.
- Austin died in 1934 at the age of 66 in Santa Fe, New Mexico.

COLOR THE POET

MAP THE POET

Locate and color Austin's state of birth, **Illinois (IL)**, on the map of the United States. Using a second shade, color the state of **California (CA)**, the location of Hunter's mountain namesake. Finally, using a third shade, color Hunter's state of death, **New Mexico (NM)**.

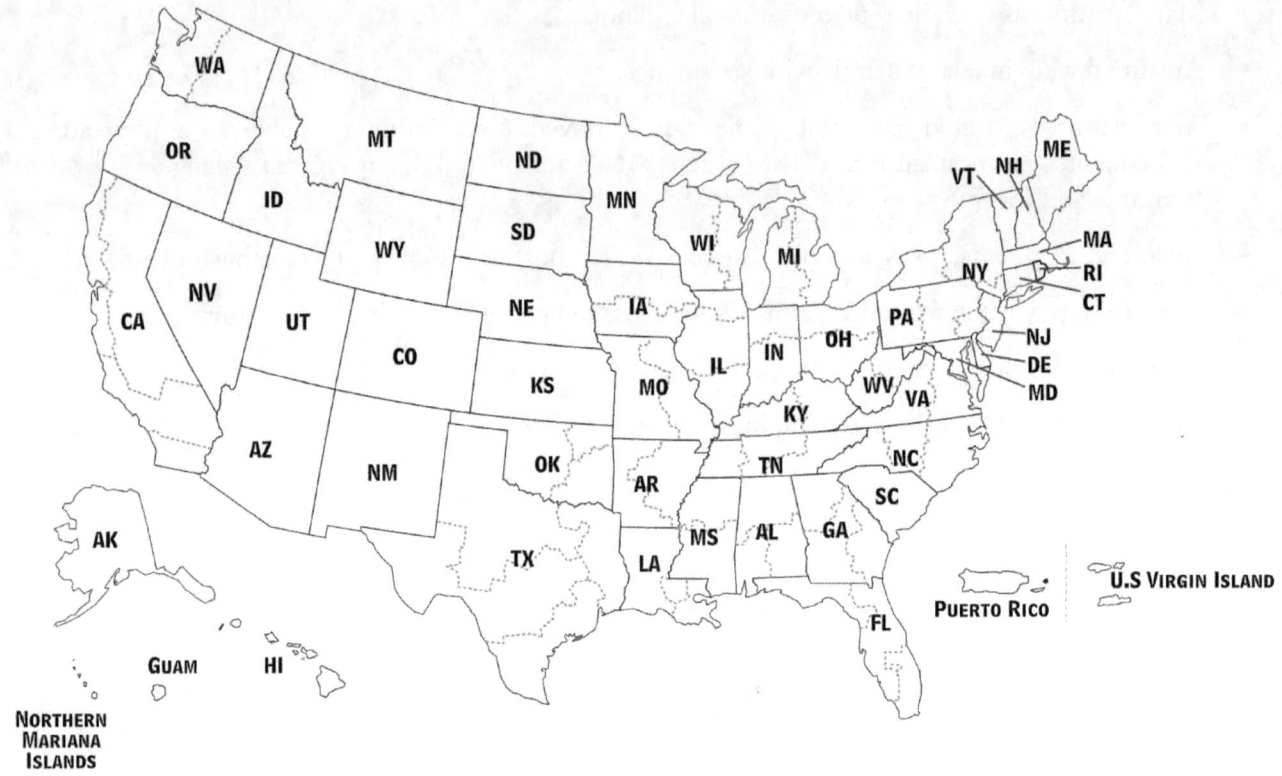

FEATURED POEM (Children Practice Reciting the Poem with Instructor Assistance.)

When misty, misty mornings come,

When wild geese low are flying,

And down along the reedy marsh

The mallard drakes are crying;

When cattle leave the highest hills,

And blackbirds flock together --

By all these signs the hunter knows

Has come good hunting weather.

SYNOPSIS

The poem lists animal behaviors that signify the beginning of hunting weather.

ENRICHMENT ACTIVITIES

1. **Recite Poem Information**
   Recite the title of the poem and the name of the poet.
2. **Narrate the Poem**
   Narrate the poem events aloud using your own words.
3. **Study the Poem Picture**
   Study the poem picture and describe how it relates to the poem.
4. **Can You Find It?**
   Find the following in the poem picture: webbed feet, feathers, and bill.
5. **Discuss Autumn Changes**
   - Mary Austin describes changes that signify good hunting weather.
   - Describe changes in flora, fauna, or weather that you would include in a poem about autumn.

VOCABULARY

Recite and Copy Each Word	Recite the Definition
reed	Any of various types of tall stiff perennial grass-like plants growing together in groups near water.
marsh	An area of low, wet land, often with tall grass.
mallard	A common and widespread duck, whose male has a distinctive dark green head.
drakes	Male ducks.
flock	A large number of birds, especially those grouped together for migration.

REVIEW QUESTIONS

1. What is the title of the poem?
2. What is the name of the poet who wrote "Hunting Weather?"
3. What happens in the poem?
4. Where does the poem take place?
5. Who are the characters in the poem?
6. What does the poem teach the reader?
7. Per the poem, which animal behaviors signify the arrival of hunting weather?

COLORING AND COPYWORK

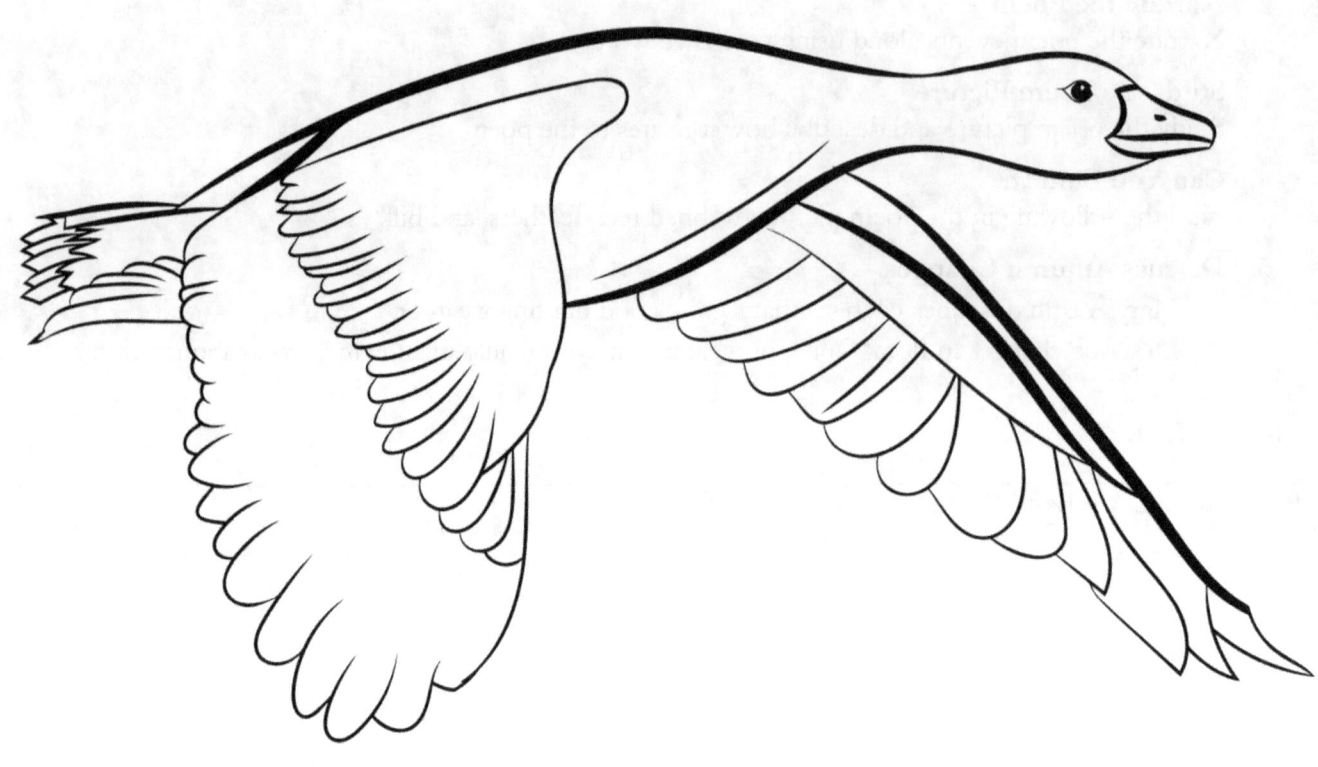

By these signs the hunter knows

Has come good hunting weather.

LESSON 10. "SIGNS OF SPRING" BY MARY AUSTIN

FEATURED POEM

Cream-cups, butter-cups,
Dandelions and sedges;
Blackbirds in the poplar row,
Sparrows in the hedges;
Fruit-buds in the orchard
Swelling with the rain;
All the close-fed pasture-lands
Growing green again.
Poppies on the river-bluff
Soon will wake from sleeping;
Home along the foothills
Woolly clouds a-creeping.

SYNOPSIS

The poem describes portents of spring including flowers growing, blackbirds and sparrows in trees and bushes, budding orchard trees, green things growing, poppies blooming, and woolly clouds creeping.

ENRICHMENT ACTIVITIES

1. **Recite Poem Information**
   Recite the title of the poem and the name of the poet.

2. **Narrate the Poem**
   Narrate the poem events aloud using your own words.

3. **Study the Poem Picture**
   Study the poem picture and describe how it relates to the poem.

4. **Can You Find It?**
   Find the following in the poem picture: beak, twig, feet, wings, and tail feathers.

5. **Discuss Signs of Spring**
   - Mary Austin describes some signs indicating the coming of spring.
   - Describe the changes in flora, fauna, or weather that you would include in a poem about spring.

VOCABULARY

Recite and Copy Each Word	Recite the Definition
sedge	Perennial herbs with long grasslike leaves, often growing in dense tufts in marshy places.
poplar	Any of various tall quick-growing deciduous trees.
orchard	A garden or an area of land for the cultivation of fruit or nut trees.
pasture	Land, specifically, an open field, on which livestock is kept for feeding.
bluff	A high, steep bank, for example by a river or the sea, or beside a ravine or plain.
foothills	Hills at the base of a mountain or mountain range.
woolly	Having a thick, soft texture, as if made of wool.

REVIEW QUESTIONS

1. What is the title of the poem?
2. What is the name of the poet who wrote "Signs of Spring?"
3. What happens in the poem?
4. Where does the poem take place?
5. Who are the characters in the poem?
6. What does the poem teach the reader?
7. Per the poem, what are the signs of spring?

COLORING AND COPYWORK

Poppies on the river-bluff

Soon will wake from sleeping.

LESSON 11. "THE SANDHILL CRANE" BY MARY AUSTIN

FEATURED POEM

Whenever the days are cool and clear,

The sandhill crane goes walking

Across the field by the flashing weir,

Slowly, solemnly stalking.

The little frogs in the tules hear,

And jump for their lives if he comes near;

The fishes scuttle away in fear

When the sandhill crane goes walking.

SYNOPSIS

When the frogs and fishes sense the sandhill crane walking, they hide to save their lives.

ENRICHMENT ACTIVITIES

1. **Recite Poem Information**
   Recite the title of the poem and the name of the poet.

2. **Narrate the Poem**
   Narrate the poem events aloud using your own words.

3. **Study the Poem Picture**
   Study the poem picture and describe how it relates to the poem.

4. **Can You Find It?**
   Find the following in the poem picture: sandhill crane, long legs, plumage, and bill.

5. **Act Out the Poem**
   - As you recite the poem, pretend to be a sandhill crane.
   - Walk around on your long legs and peer intently at the meadows and streams for frogs and fishes.
   - Spot a frog and snatch him up with your long, pointed bill.

VOCABULARY

Recite and Copy Each Word	Recite the Definition
crane	Large birds with long legs and a long neck which is extended during flight.
weir	An adjustable dam placed across a river to regulate the flow of water downstream.
solemnly	In a deeply serious manner.
stalking	Walking behind something, such as a screen, for the purpose of approaching game; to proceed under cover.
tules	Giant, grasslike plants that grow on marshy lands.
scuttle	To move hastily or to scurry.

REVIEW QUESTIONS

1. What is the title of the poem?
2. What is the name of the poet who wrote "The Sandhill Crane?"
3. What happens in the poem?
4. Where does the poem take place?
5. Who are the characters in the poem?
6. What does the poem teach the reader?
7. Why do the frogs and fishes hide from the sandhill crane?

COLORING AND COPYWORK

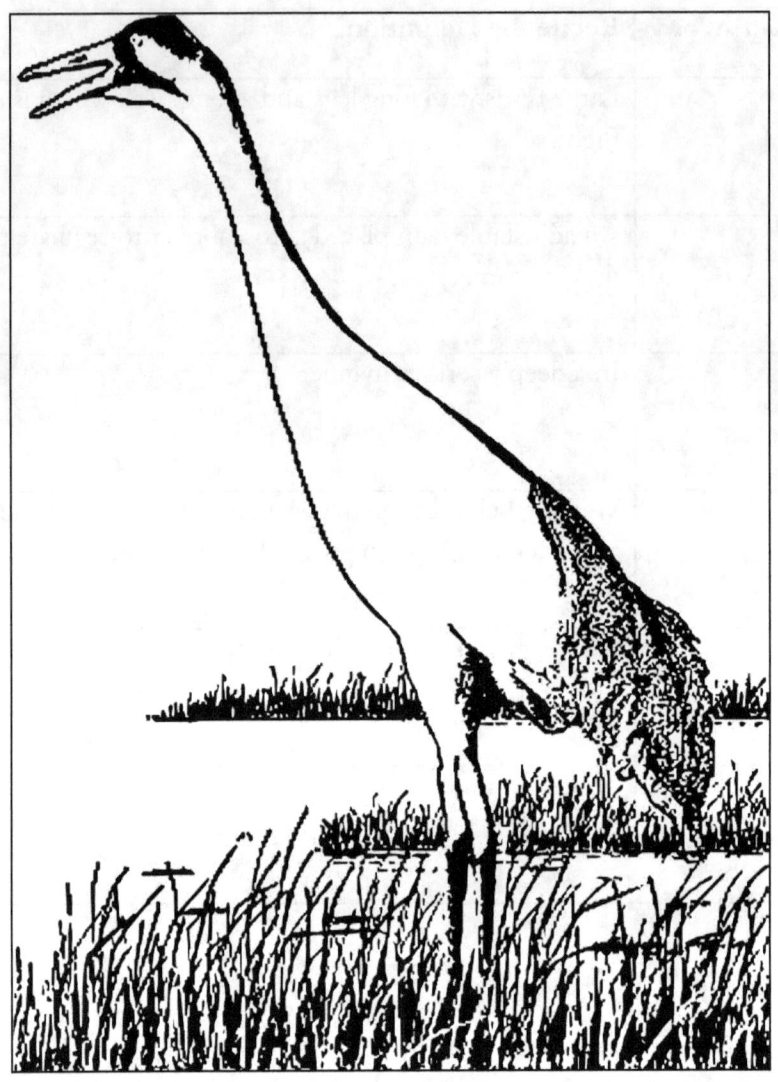

Whenever the days are clear,

The sandhill crane goes walking.

LESSON 12. "BLUE-EYED GRASS" BY MARY AUSTIN

FEATURED POEM

Blue-eyed grass in the meadow
And yarrow-blooms on the hill,
Cattails that rustle and whisper,
And winds that are never still;

Blue-eyed grass in the meadow,
A linnet's nest near by,
Blackbirds caroling clearly
Somewhere between earth and sky;

Blue-eyed grass in the meadow,
And the laden bee's low hum,
Milkweeds all by the roadside,
To tell us summer is come.

SYNOPSIS

The poem describes the sights and sounds that signify the arrival of summer.

ENRICHMENT ACTIVITIES

1. **Recite Poem Information**
   Recite the title of the poem and the name of the poet.

2. **Narrate the Poem**
   Narrate the poem events aloud using your own words.

3. **Study the Poem Picture**
   Study the poem picture and describe how it relates to the poem.

4. **Can You Find It?**
   Find the following in the poem picture: blue-eyed grass, blossoms, petals, stems, and leaves.

VOCABULARY

Recite and Copy Each Word	Recite the Definition
yarrow	A plant of the daisy family, with feathery leaves and heads of small white, yellow, or pink aromatic flowers.
cattail	A tall, reed-like marsh plant with strap-like leaves and a dark brown, velvety cylindrical head of numerous tiny flowers.
linnet	A mainly brown and gray bird with a reddish breast and forehead.
laden	Heavily loaded or weighed down.
milkweed	A herbaceous American plant with milky sap.

REVIEW QUESTIONS

1. What is the title of the poem?
2. What is the name of the poet who wrote "Signs of Spring?"
3. What happens in the poem?
4. Where does the poem take place?
5. Who are the characters in the poem?
6. What does the poem teach the reader?
7. Per the poem, what are the signs of spring?

ELEMENTARY POETRY VOLUME 3: POETRY OF NATURE, REVELRY, AND RHYME

COLORING AND COPYWORK

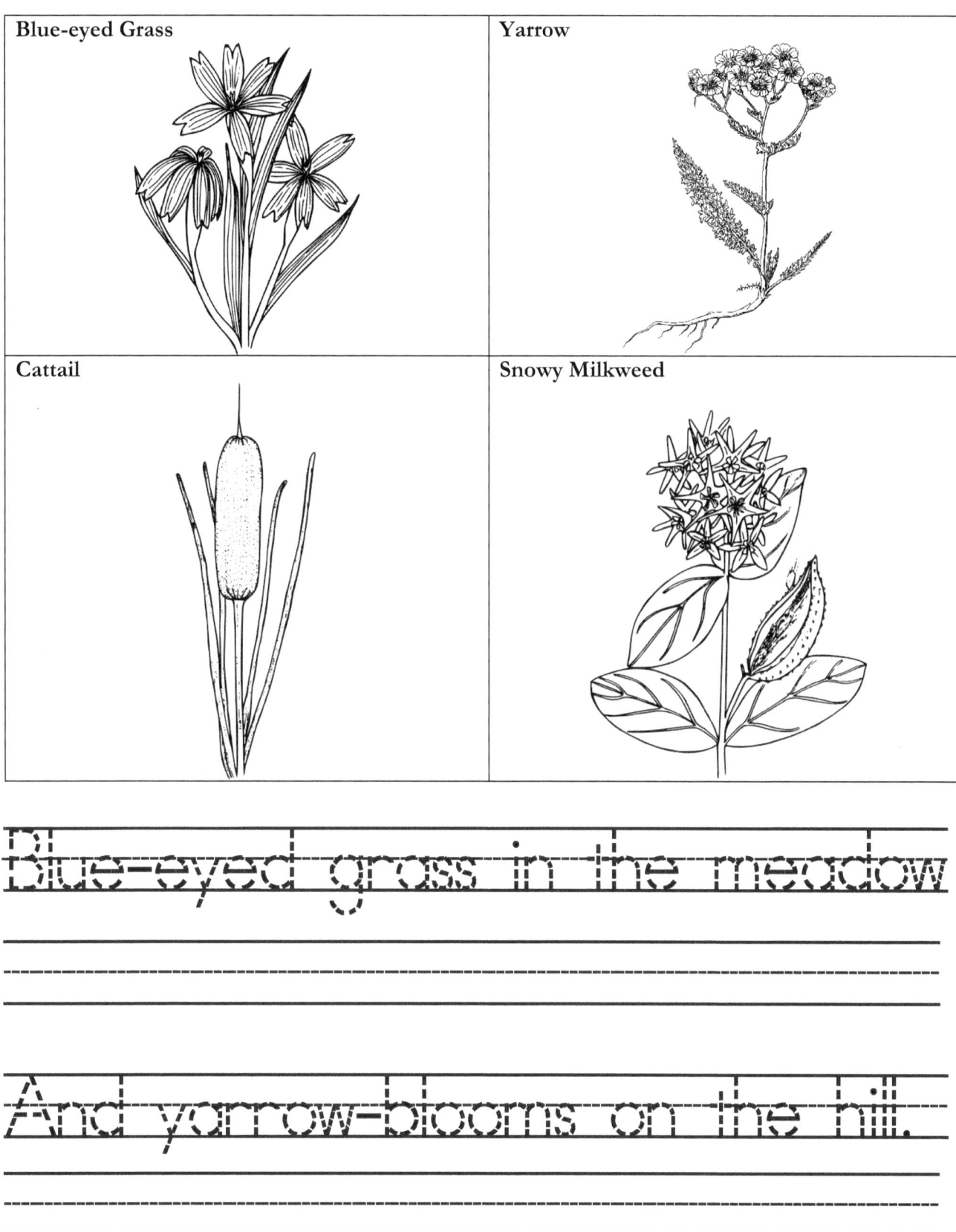

Blue-eyed grass in the meadow

And yarrow-blooms on the hill.

LESSON 13. "PRAIRIE-DOG TOWN"
BY MARY AUSTIN

FEATURED POEM

1. Old Peter Prairie-Dog
Builds him a house
In Prairie-Dog Town,
With a door that goes down
And down and down,
And a hall that goes under
And under and under,
Where you can't see the lightning,
You can't hear the thunder,
For they don't like thunder
In Prairie-Dog Town.

2. Old Peter Prairie-Dog
Digs him a cellar
In Prairie-Dog Town,
With a ceiling that is arched
And a wall that is round,
And the earth he takes out he makes into a mound.
And the hall and the cellar
Are dark as dark,
And you can't see a spark,
Not a single spark;
And the way to them cannot be found.

3. Old Peter Prairie-Dog
Knows a very clever trick
Of behaving like a stick
When he hears a sudden sound,
Like an old dead stick;
And when you turn your head
He'll jump quick, quick,
And be another stick
When you look around.
It is a clever trick,
And it keeps him safe and sound
In the cellar and the halls
That are under the mound
In Prairie-Dog Town.

SYNOPSIS

Peter Prairie-Dog builds an underground house in Prairie-Dog Town. His underground house is dark and quiet. When he sees anyone above ground, he stays still and upright like a stick to protect himself and his home.

ENRICHMENT ACTIVITIES

1. **Recite Poem Information**
   Recite the title of the poem and the name of the poet.
2. **Narrate the Poem**
   Narrate the poem events aloud using your own words.
3. **Study the Poem Picture**
   Study the poem picture and describe how it relates to the poem.
4. **Can You Find It?**
   Find the following in the poem picture: tail, claws, whiskers, and ears.
5. **Act Out the Poem**
   - Pretend to be Peter Prairie-Dog.
   - Pop out of your hole and glance around.
   - Spot a stranger and stand still and upright like a stick.

VOCABULARY

Recite and Copy Each Word	Recite the Definition
prairie dog	A small, stout-bodied burrowing rodent with shallow cheek pouches.
cellar	An enclosed underground space, often under a building, used for storage or shelter.
arch	An inverted U shape.
mound	An artificial hill or elevation of earth.
spark	A small particle of glowing matter, either molten or on fire.

REVIEW QUESTIONS

1. What is the title of the poem?
2. What is the name of the poet who wrote "Prairie-Dog Town?"
3. What happens in the poem?
4. Where does the poem take place?
5. Who are the characters in the poem?
6. What does the poem teach the reader?
7. What does Peter Prairie-Dog do when he sees anyone above ground?

COLORING AND COPYWORK

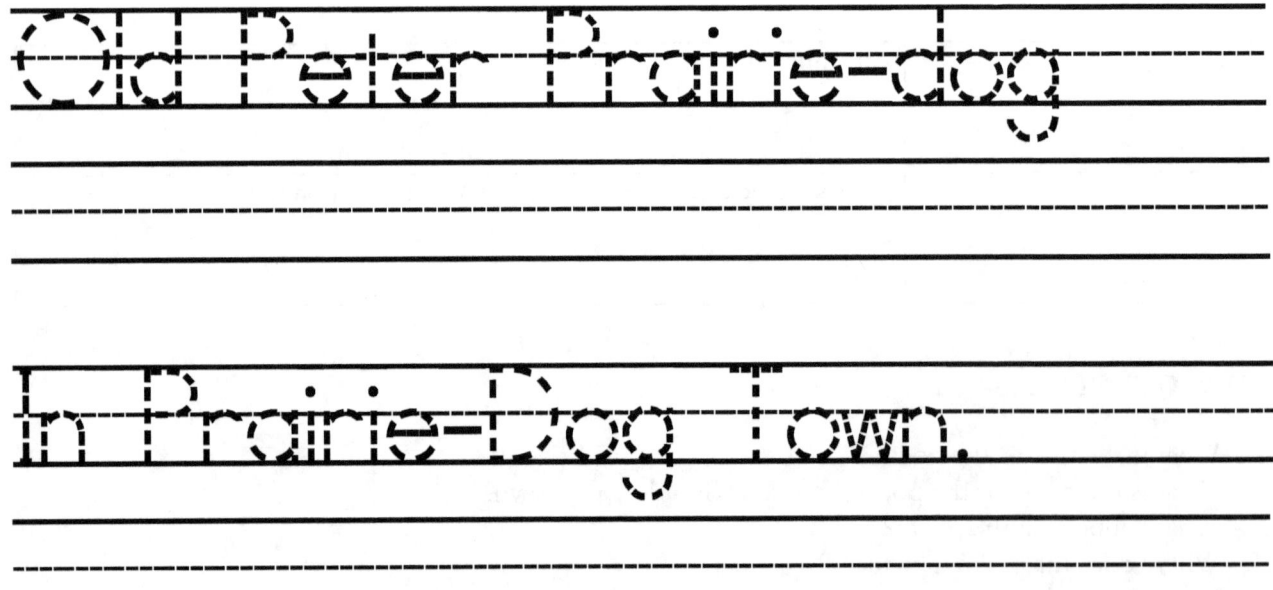

Old Peter Prairie-dog

In Prairie-Dog Town.

POET IV: EUGENE FIELD
LESSON 14. "WYNKEN, BLYNKEN, AND NOD"

POET OVERVIEW

- Eugene Field was born in 1850 in Saint Louis, Illinois.
- Field was afraid of the dark as a boy.
- His mother died when he was six, and his father sent him to live on his cousin's farm.
- Field wrote his first poem on the farm about his cousin's dog, Fido.
- Field married young and had eight children, but only five survived beyond childhood.
- Field published poems beginning in 1879, when he was 29.
- Field died of a heart attack at the age of 45 in Chicago, Illinois.

COLOR THE POET

MAP THE POET

Locate and color Field's state of birth and death, **Illinois (IL)**, on the map of the United States.

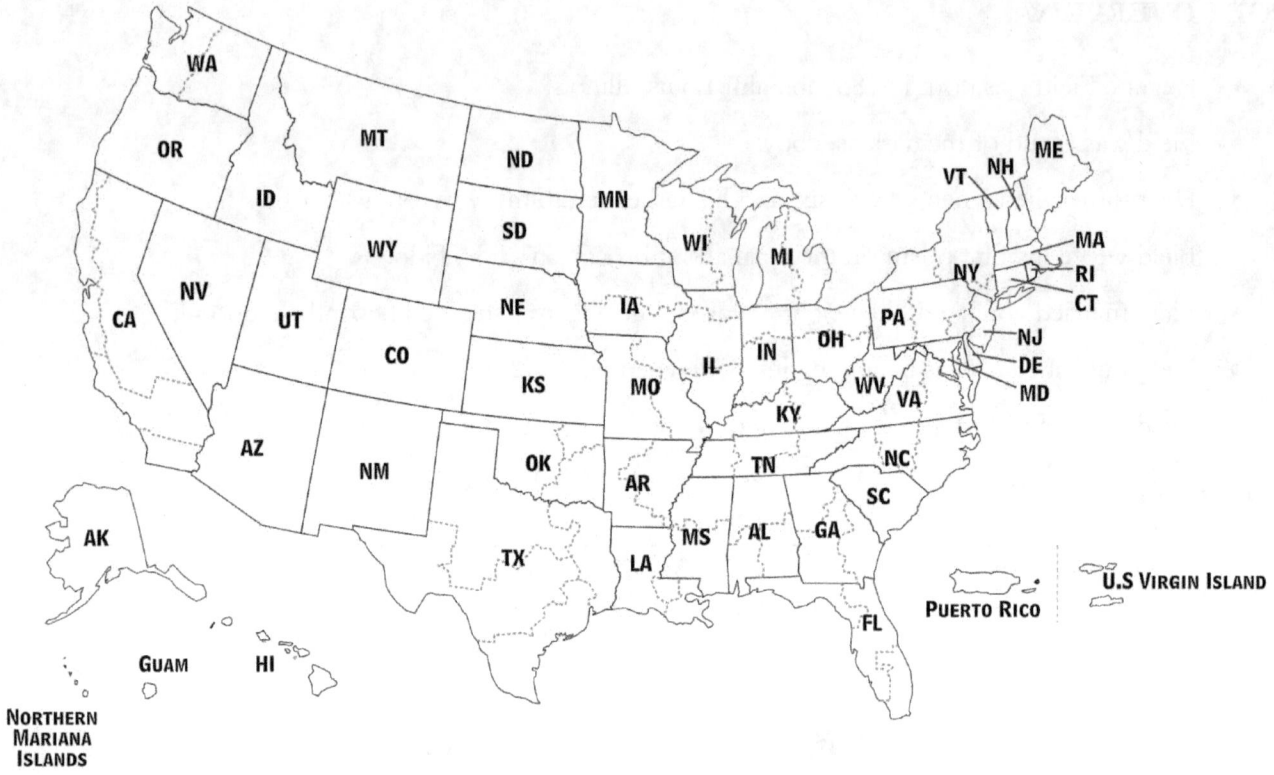

FEATURED POEM (Children Practice Reciting the Poem with Instructor Assistance.)

1. Wynken, Blynken, and Nod one night

Sailed off in a wooden shoe,--

Sailed on a river of crystal light,

Into a sea of dew.

"Where are you going, and what do you wish?"

The old moon asked the three.

"We have come to fish for the herring-fish

That live in this beautiful sea;

Nets of silver and gold have we,"

Said Wynken, Blynken, And Nod.

2. The old moon laughed and sang a song,

As they rocked in the wooden shoe;

And the wind that sped them all night long

Ruffled the waves of dew;

The little stars were the herring-fish

That lived in that beautiful sea.

"Now cast your nets wherever you wish,--

Never afraid are we!"

So cried the stars to the fishermen three,

Wynken, Blynken, And Nod.

3. All night long their nets they threw

To the stars in the twinkling foam,--

Then down from the skies came the wooden shoe,

Bringing the fishermen home:

'Twas all so pretty a sail, it seemed

As if it could not be;

And some folks thought 'twas a dream they'd dreamed

Of sailing that beautiful sea;

But I shall name you the fishermen three:

Wynken, Blynken, And Nod.

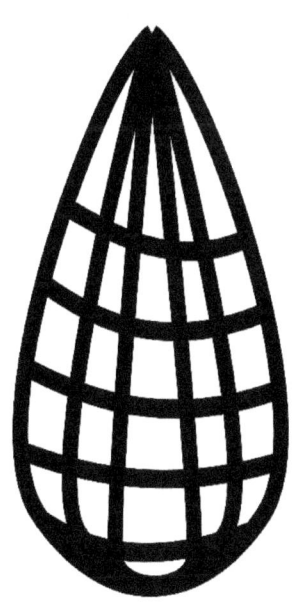

4. Wynken and Blynken are two little eyes,

And Nod is a little head,

And the wooden shoe that sailed the skies

Is a wee one's trundle-bed;

So shut your eyes while Mother sings

Of wonderful sights that be,

And you shall see the beautiful things

As you rock in the misty sea

Where the old shoe rocked the fishermen three:--

Wynken, Blynken, And Nod

SYNOPSIS

Wynken, Blynken, and Nod ride in a wooden shoe to fish in a beautiful sea. In the final stanza, the poem reveals Wynken and Blynken are the eyes of a sleeping child, Nod is the child's head, and the wooden shoe is the child's bed.

ENRICHMENT ACTIVITIES

1. **Recite Poem Information**
   Recite the title of the poem and the name of the poet.
2. **Narrate the Poem**
   Narrate the poem events aloud using your own words.
3. **Study the Poem Pictures**
   Study the poem pictures and describe how they relate to the poem.
4. **Can You Find It?**
   Find the following in the poem pictures: Wynken, Blynken, Nod, wooden shoe, moon, herring, fishing net, and sleeping child.

VOCABULARY

Recite and Copy Each Word	Recite the Definition
crystal	A highly transparent glass.
dew	Moisture in the air that settles on plants or other items in the morning, resulting in drops.
herring	A type of small, oily fish often used as food.
ruffled	Disturbed or agitated.
foam	A substance composed of a large collection of bubbles or their solidified remains.
trundle-bed	A low bed, designed to be rolled/stored away, usually on casters, under a higher bed.

REVIEW QUESTIONS

1. What is the title of the poem?
2. What is the name of the poet who wrote "Wynken, Blynken, and Nod?"
3. What happens in the poem?
4. Where does the poem take place?
5. Who are the characters in the poem?
6. What does the poem teach the reader?

COLORING AND COPYWORK

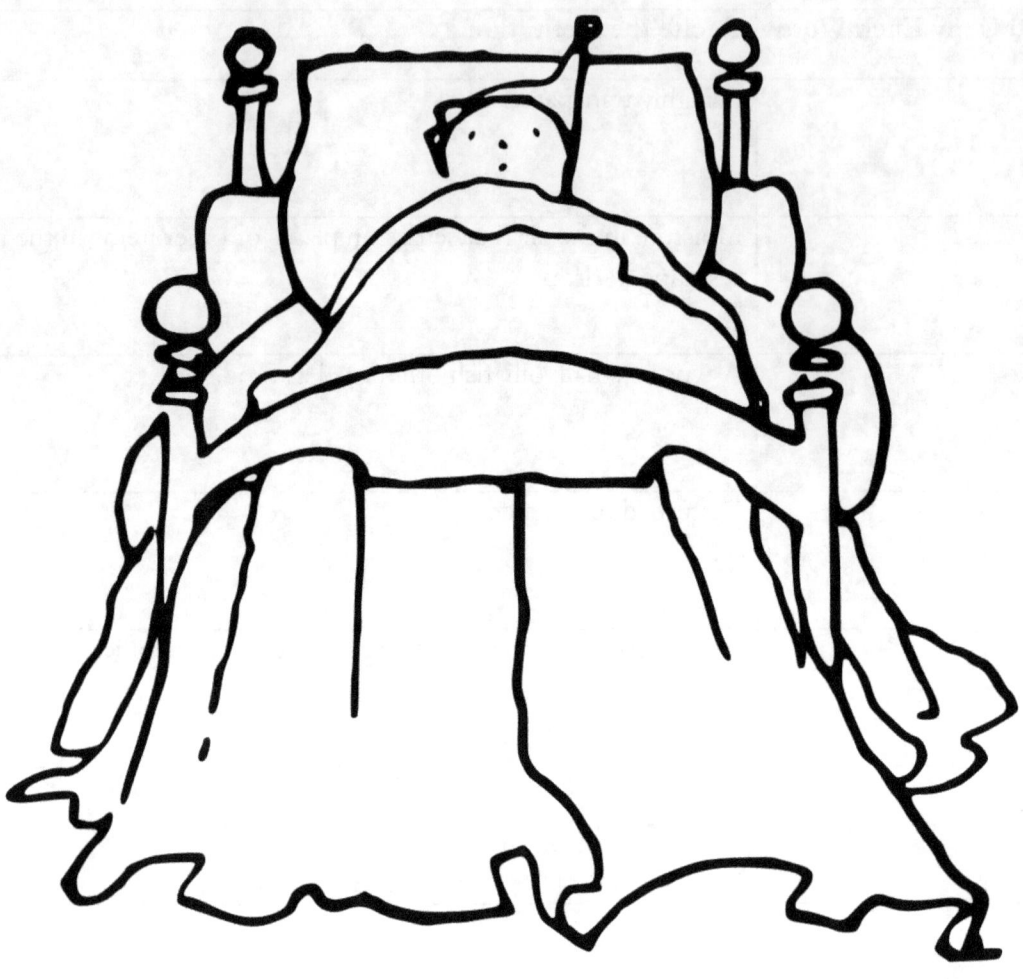

Wynken, Blynken, and Nod

Sailed off in a wooden shoe.

LESSON 15. "LITTLE BLUE PIGEON"
BY EUGENE FIELD

FEATURED POEM

Sleep, little pigeon, and fold your wings,--
Little blue pigeon with velvet eyes;
Sleep to the singing of mother-bird swinging--
Swinging the nest where her little one lies.

Away out yonder I see a star,--
Silvery star with a tinkling song;
To the soft dew falling I hear it calling--
Calling and tinkling the night along.

In through the window a moonbeam comes,--
Little gold moonbeam with misty wings;
All silently creeping, it asks, "Is he sleeping--
Sleeping and dreaming while mother sings?"

Up from the sea there floats the sob
Of the waves that are breaking upon the shore,
As though they were groaning in anguish, and moaning--
Bemoaning the ship that shall come no more.

But sleep, little pigeon, and fold your wings,--
Little blue pigeon with mournful eyes;
Am I not singing?--see, I am swinging--
Swinging the nest where my darling lies.

SYNOPSIS

A lullaby poem describes the beauty of the night and encourages "little pigeons" to sleep.

ENRICHMENT ACTIVITIES

1. **Recite Poem Information**
   Recite the title of the poem and the name of the poet.

2. **Narrate the Poem**
   Narrate the poem events aloud using your own words.

3. **Study the Poem Picture**
   Study the poem picture and describe how it relates to the poem.

4. **Can You Find It?**
    Find the following in the poem picture: little girl, little pigeon, bed, pillow, and covers.

VOCABULARY

Recite and Copy Each Word	Recite the Definition
pigeon	A stout bird with gray and white feathers that makes a cooing call.
velvet	A soft fabric with a thick short pile on one side.
yonder	Distant but within sight.
moonbeam	A shaft of moonlight.
anguish	To suffer pain.
mournful	Filled with grief or sadness.
darling	A person who is dear or cherished.

REVIEW QUESTIONS

1. What is the title of the poem?
2. What is the name of the poet who wrote "Little Blue Pigeon?"
3. What happens in the poem?
4. Where does the poem take place?
5. Who are the characters in the poem?
6. What does the poem teach the reader?

COLORING AND COPYWORK

LITTLE BLUE PIGEON.

Away out yonder I see a star,

Silvery star with a tinkling song

LESSON 16. "THE SUGAR PLUM TREE" BY EUGENE FIELD

FEATURED POEM

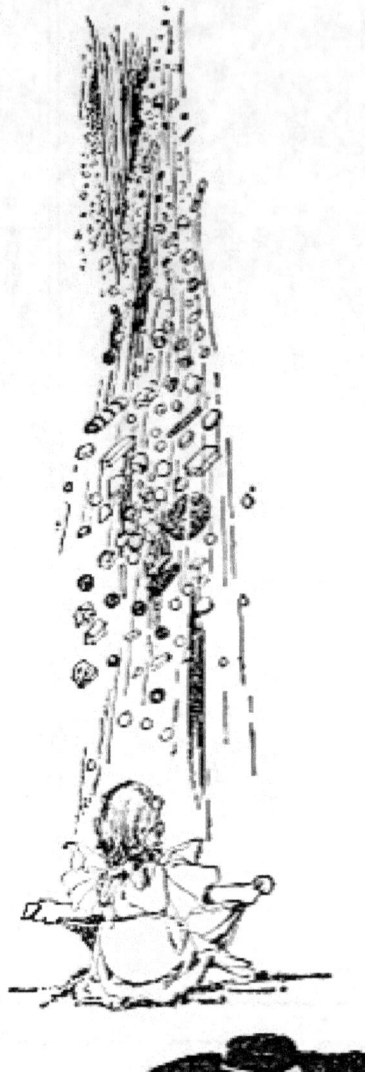

Have you ever heard of the Sugar-Plum Tree?
'Tis a marvel of great renown!
It blooms on the shore of the Lollypop sea
In the garden of Shut-Eye Town;
The fruit that it bears is so wondrously sweet
(As those who have tasted it say)
That good little children have only to eat
Of that fruit to be happy next day.

When you've got to the tree, you would have a hard time
To capture the fruit which I sing;
The tree is so tall that no person could climb
To the boughs where the sugar-plums swing!
But up in that tree sits a chocolate cat,
And a gingerbread dog prowls below -
And this is the way you contrive to get at
Those sugar-plums tempting you so:

You say but the word to that gingerbread dog
And he barks with terrible zest
That the chocolate cat is at once all agog,
As her swelling proportions attest.
And the chocolate cat goes cavorting around
From this leafy limb unto that,
And the sugar-plums tumble, of course, to the ground -
Hurrah for that chocolate cat!

There are marshmallows, gumdrops, and peppermint canes,
With stripings of scarlet or gold,
And you carry away of the treasure that rains,
As much as your apron can hold!
So come, little child, cuddle closer to me
In your dainty white nightcap and gown,
And I'll rock you away to that Sugar-Plum Tree
In the garden of Shut-Eye Town.

SYNOPSIS

The lovely Sugar-Plum Tree grows delicious sweets that make children happy. The tree is too tall for people to reach the candy. To get the candy, people must ask the gingerbread dog below the tree to bark, which scares the chocolate cat in the tree into knocking down the candy.

ENRICHMENT ACTIVITIES

1. **Recite Poem Information**
   Recite the title of the poem and the name of the poet.

2. **Narrate the Poem**
   Narrate the poem events aloud using your own words.

3. **Study the Poem Picture**
   Study the poem picture and describe how it relates to the poem.

4. **Can You Find It?**
   Find the following in the poem picture: little girl, hat, and cascading candy.

VOCABULARY

Recite and Copy Each Word	Recite the Definition
renown	Fame, celebrity, or wide recognition.
wondrously	In an amazing, marvelous, or awe-inspiring manner.
boughs	Firm branches of a tree.
contrive	To plan, scheme, or plot.
zest	Enthusiasm, keen enjoyment, relish, or gusto.
agog	In a state of high anticipation, excitement, or interest.
cavorting	Moving about carelessly, playfully, or boisterously.

REVIEW QUESTIONS

1. What is the title of the poem?
2. What is the name of the poet who wrote "The Sugar Plum Tree?"
3. What happens in the poem?
4. Where does the poem take place?
5. Who are the characters in the poem?
6. What does the poem teach the reader?

COLORING AND COPYWORK

In the tree sits a chocolate cat

A gingerbread dog prowls below.

LESSON 17. "THE DUEL"
BY EUGENE FIELD

FEATURED POEM

1. The gingham dog and the calico cat
Side by side on the table sat;
'T was half-past twelve, and (what do you think!)
Nor one nor t' other had slept a wink!
The old Dutch clock and the Chinese plate
Appeared to know as sure as fate
There was going to be a terrible spat.
(I wasn't there; I simply state
What was told to me by the Chinese plate!)

2. The gingham dog went "bow-wow-wow!"
And the calico cat replied "mee-ow!"
The air was littered, an hour or so,
With bits of gingham and calico,
While the old Dutch clock in the chimney place
Up with its hands before its face,
For it always dreaded a family row!
(Now mind: I'm only telling you
What the old Dutch clock declares is true!)

3. The Chinese plate looked very blue,
And wailed, "Oh, dear! what shall we do!"
But the gingham dog and the calico cat
Wallowed this way and tumbled that,
Employing every tooth and claw
In the awfullest way you ever saw -
And, oh! how the gingham and calico flew!
(Don't fancy I exaggerate -
I got my news from the Chinese plate!)

4. Next morning, where the two had sat
They found no trace of dog or cat;
And some folks think unto this day
That burglars stole that pair away!
But the truth about the cat and pup
Is this: they ate each other up!
Now what do you really think of that!
(The old Dutch clock it told me so,
And that is how I came to know.)

SYNOPSIS

An old Dutch clock and a Chinese plate tell the narrator a terrible tale about a battle between a gingham dog and a calico cat. Neither the cat nor the dog wins their fight. Instead, both the dog and cat disappear forever, having eaten each other up.

ENRICHMENT ACTIVITIES

1. **Recite Poem Information**
   Recite the title of the poem and the name of the poet.
2. **Narrate the Poem**
   Narrate the poem events aloud using your own words.
3. **Study the Poem Picture**
   Study the poem picture and describe how it relates to the poem.
4. **Can You Find It?**
   Find the following in the poem picture: gingham dog, calico cat, table, clock, and poem title.

VOCABULARY

Recite and Copy Each Word	Recite the Definition
gingham	A cotton fabric made from dyed and white yarn woven in checks.
calico	1. A kind of rough cloth, often printed with a bright pattern. 2. A cat with fur of the colors black, white and orange.
Dutch	Of or pertaining to the Netherlands.
Chinese	Of or pertaining to China.
spat	A brief argument, falling out, or quarrel.
wallowed	Rolled about in something dirty, for example in mud.

REVIEW QUESTIONS

1. What is the title of the poem?
2. What is the name of the poet who wrote "The Duel?"
3. What happens in the poem?
4. Where does the poem take place?
5. Who are the characters in the poem?
6. What does the poem teach the reader?

COLORING AND COPYWORK

The gingham dog went "bow-wow!"

The calico cat replied "mee-ow!"

LESSON 18. "JEST 'FORE CHRISTMAS" BY EUGENE FIELD

FEATURED POEM

Father calls me William, sister calls me Will,
Mother calls me Willie, but the fellers call me Bill!
Mighty glad I ain't a girl - ruther be a boy,
Without them sashes, curls, an' things that's worn by Fauntleroy!
Love to chawnk green apples an' go swimmin' in the lake -
Hate to take the castor-ile they give for bellyache!
'Most all the time, the whole year round, there ain't no flies on me,
But jest 'fore Christmas I'm as good as I kin be!

Got a yeller dog named Sport, sick him on the cat;
First thing she knows she doesn't know where she is at!
Got a clipper sled, an' when us kids goes out to slide,
'Long comes the grocery cart, an' we all hook a ride!
But sometimes when the grocery man is worrited an' cross,
He reaches at us with his whip, an' larrups up his hoss,
An' then I laff an' holler, "Oh, ye never teched me!"
But jest 'fore Christmas I'm as good as I kin be!

Gran'ma says she hopes that when I git to be a man,
I'll be a missionarer like her oldest brother, Dan,
As was et up by the cannibuls that lives in Ceylon's Isle,
Where every prospeck pleases, an' only man is vile!
But gran'ma she has never been to see a Wild West show,
Nor read the Life of Daniel Boone, or else I guess she'd know
That Buff'lo Bill an' cow-boys is good enough for me!
Excep' jest 'fore Christmas, when I'm good as I kin be!

And then old Sport he hangs around, so solemn-like an' still,
His eyes they seem a-sayin': "What's the matter, little Bill?"
The old cat sneaks down off her perch an' wonders what's become
Of them two enemies of hern that used to make things hum!
But I am so perlite an' 'tend so earnestly to biz,
That mother says to father: "How improved our Willie is!"
But father, havin' been a boy hisself, suspicions me
When, jest 'fore Christmas, I'm as good as I kin be!

For Christmas, with its lots an' lots of candies, cakes, an' toys,
Was made, they say, for proper kids an' not for naughty boys;
So wash yer face an' bresh yer hair, an' mind yer p's and q's,
An' don't bust out yer pantaloons, and don't wear out yer shoes;
Say "Yessum" to the ladies, an' "Yessur" to the men,
An' when they's company, don't pass yer plate for pie again;
But, thinkin' of the things yer'd like to see upon that tree,
Jest 'fore Christmas be as good as yer kin be!

SYNOPSIS

The poem narrator discusses how he is a mischievous troublemaker throughout the year with one exception - he's extra good right before Christmas to ensure he receives presents under the tree.

ENRICHMENT ACTIVITIES

1. **Recite Poem Information**
   Recite the title of the poem and the name of the poet.

2. **Narrate the Poem**
   Narrate the poem events aloud using your own words.

3. **Study the Poem Picture**
   Study the poem picture and describe how it relates to the poem.

4. **Can You Find It?**
   Find the following in the poem picture: bells, Santa Claus, little boy, holly, Santa's sack, and toys.

5. **Map the Poem**
   - The narrator mentions his great uncle was a missionary in Ceylon's Isle, the present-day island of Sri Lanka.
   - Study the map of south-central Asia below and find Sri Lanka. Color Sri Lanka green.
   - Which shape does Sri Lanka most closely resemble – a circle, square, oval, tear drop, or triangle?
   - Which ocean surrounds the island of Sri Lanka? Color the ocean blue.
   - Which large country is near Sri Lanka?

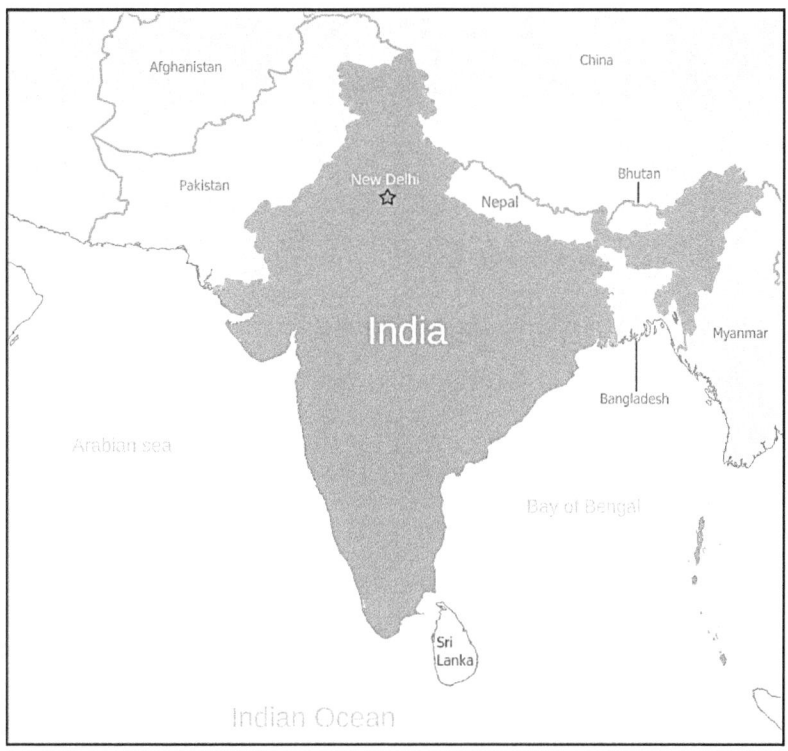

6. **Explore Wild West Shows**
    - The poem narrator expresses admiration for Buffalo Bill, who was an 1800s-era guide, pony express rider, buffalo hunter, and showman from the wild west of America.
    - Buffalo Bill and his rough riders toured the United States and Europe and put on Wild West Shows featuring settlers, cowboys, buffalos, and American Indians.
    - Find the following in the Buffalo Bill poster: Buffalo Bill, cowboys, cowboy hats, handkerchiefs, boots, gun holster, rearing horse, galloping horse, manes, saddle, bridle, stirrup, cattle, and lasso.

VOCABULARY

Recite and Copy Each Word	Recite the Definition
Fauntleroy	A fussily adorned young boy.
chawnk (chuck)	A casual throw.
castor-ile (castor oil)	The pale-yellow vegetable oil extracted from the castor bean, used to provoke vomiting.
clipper sled	A type of wooden snow sled with metal rails.

Recite and Copy Each Word	Recite the Definition
laff	Laugh.
larrup	To beat or thrash.
missionarer (missionary)	A person who travels attempting to spread a religion or a creed.
cannibuls (cannibals)	An organism which eats others of its own species, especially a human who eats human flesh.
Ceylon's Isle	An archaic name for *Sri Lanka*.
prospeck (prospect)	A picturesque or panoramic view.
vile	Morally low, base, or despicable.
Wild West Show	A show featuring fictionalized scenes and events from the American western frontier (e.g. cowboys on horses, American Indians, herding cattle).
Daniel Boone	An American frontiersman who explored and established a settlement on land that is now Kentucky.
Buff'lo Bill (Buffalo Bill)	An 1800s-era guide, pony express rider, buffalo hunter, and showman from the wild west of America.
perlite (polite)	Well-mannered or civilized.
bresh	Brush.
pantaloons	An article of clothing covering each leg separately, that covers the area from the waist to the ankle.

REVIEW QUESTIONS

1. What is the title of the poem?
2. What is the name of the poet who wrote "Jest 'Fore Christmas?"
3. What happens in the poem?
4. Who are the characters in the poem?
5. What does the poem teach the reader?

COLORING AND COPYWORK

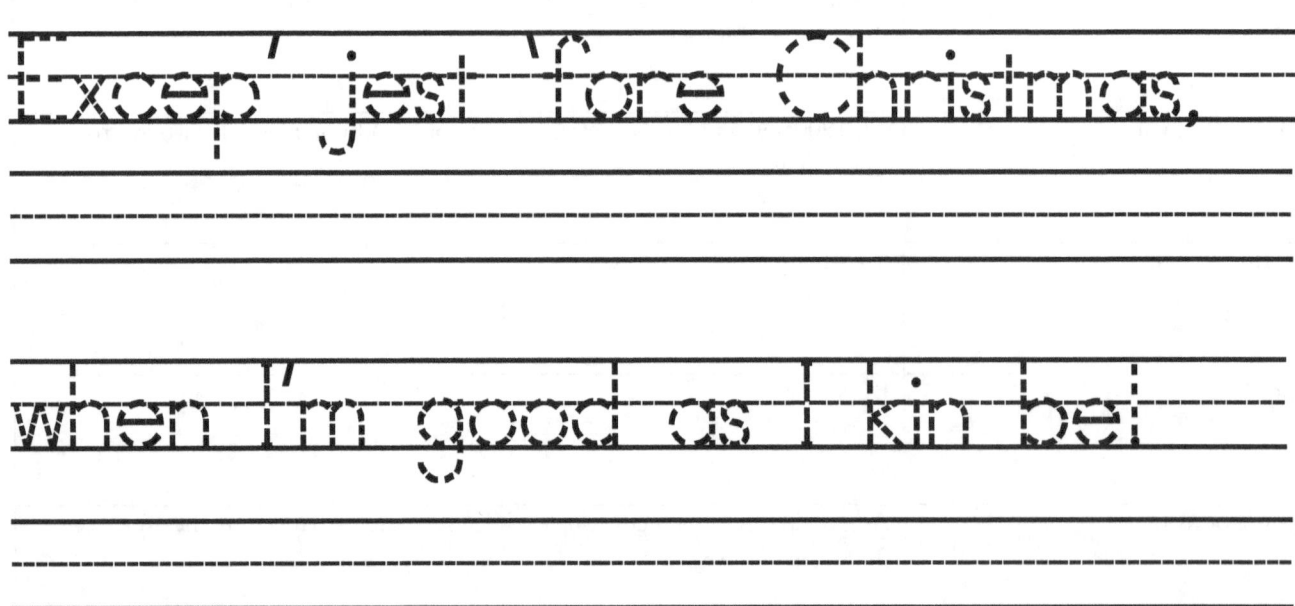

Excep' jest 'fore Christmas,

when I'm good as I kin be!

POET V: ROBERT LOUIS STEVENSON
LESSON 19. "FIFTEEN MEN ON THE DEAD MAN'S CHEST"

POET OVERVIEW

- Robert Louis Stevenson was born in 1850 in Edinburgh, Scotland.
- Although his family was in the business of engineering lighthouses, Stevenson wanted to write from an early age.
- Stevenson spent much of his life traveling around the world.
- In addition to poetry, Stevenson wrote famous books such as "Treasure Island," "Kidnapped," and "Strange Case of Dr. Jekyll and Mr. Hyde."
- Stevenson died in 1894 at the age of 44 in the Samoan Islands.

COLOR THE POET

MAP THE POET

Locate and color Stevenson's country of birth, **Scotland** (Northern United Kingdom), on the map of Europe.

FEATURED POEM (Children Practice Reciting the Poem with Instructor Assistance.)

Fifteen men on the Dead Man's Chest —
Yo-ho-ho, and a bottle of rum!
Drink and the devil had done for the rest —
Yo-ho-ho, and a bottle of rum!

SYNOPSIS

The poem is a sea song found Robert Louis Stevenson's book "Treasure Island." For many years, no one knew what Stevenson meant by the song. The hypothesis offered in "Geographical", a publication of the Royal Geographical Society, is that the famous pirate, Blackbeard, marooned his misbehaving crew on the island of Dead Man's Chest in the British Virgin Islands. Blackbeard gave each crew member a bottle of rum and a sword. The island had little water or food. Blackbeard hoped the men would die, but when Blackbeard returned 30 days later, 15 of the men were still alive.

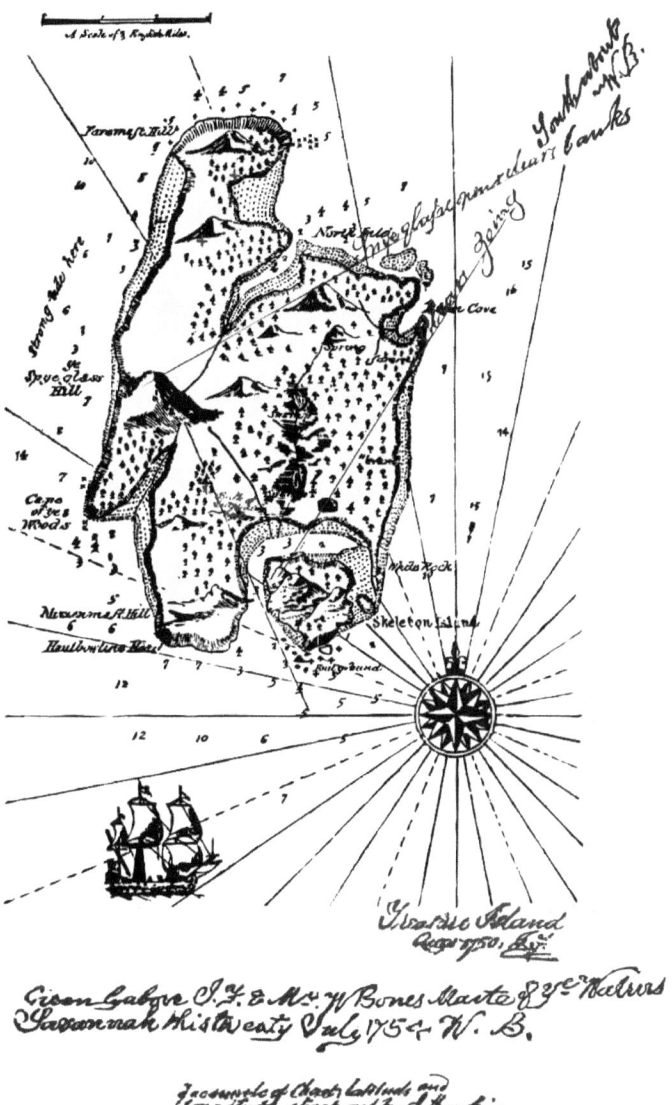

ENRICHMENT ACTIVITIES

1. **Recite Poem Information**
   Recite the title of the poem and the name of the poet.

2. **Narrate the Poem**
   Narrate the poem events aloud using your own words.

3. **Study the Poem Picture**
   Study the poem picture and describe how it relates to the poem.

4. **Can You Find It?**
   Find the following in the poem picture: island, pirate ship, and compass.

5. **Play Pirate Hide-and-Seek**
   - Have each person secretly hide a "treasure" indoors or outdoors and draw a map to the treasure. Make sure people do not know where other people's treasures are hidden.
   - "Treasure" might be anything: a toy, a small bag of pennies, a certain colored crayon, etc.
   - Exchange maps and see who can follow their map to find the related treasure.

6. **Map the Poem**
    - Dead Man's Chest is an island in the British Virgin Islands.
    - Find the British Virgin Islands on the map of the Caribbean.

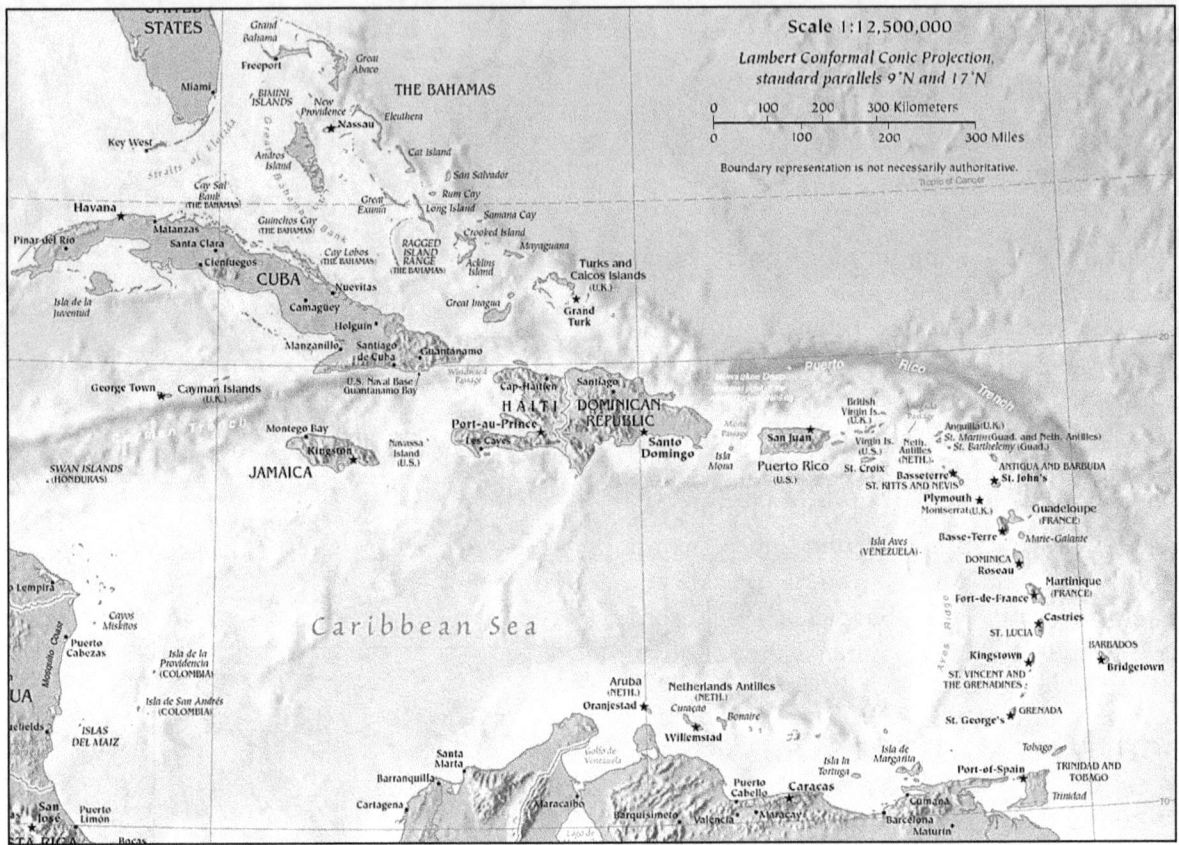

VOCABULARY

Recite and Copy Each Word	Recite the Definition
Dead Man's Chest	An island in the British Virgin Islands.
Yo-ho-ho	A saying associated with pirates and seafaring.

REVIEW QUESTIONS

1. What is the title of the poem?
2. What is the name of the poet who wrote "Fifteen Men on the Dead Man's Chest?"
3. What happens in the poem?
4. Where does the poem take place?
5. Who are the characters in the poem?

COLORING AND COPYWORK

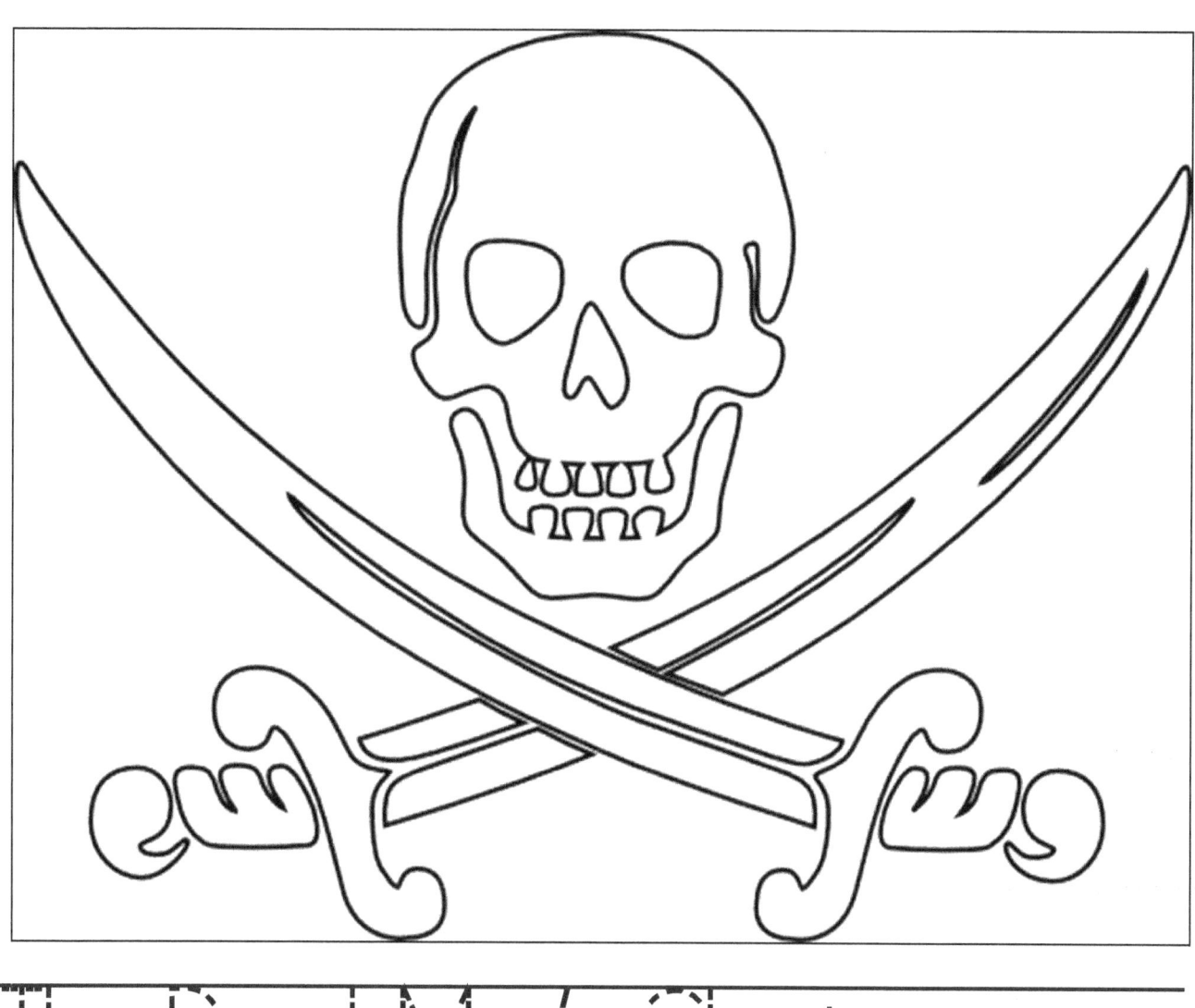

The Dead Man's Chest

Yo-ho-ho, and a bottle of rum!

LESSON 20. "A GOOD BOY" BY ROBERT LOUIS STEVENSON

FEATURED POEM (Children Practice Reciting the Poem with Instructor Assistance.)

I woke before the morning, I was happy all the day,
I never said an ugly word, but smiled and stuck to play.

And now at last the sun is going down behind the wood,
And I am very happy, for I know that I've been good.

My bed is waiting cool and fresh, with linen smooth and fair,
And I must be off to sleepsin-by, and not forget my prayer.

I know that, till tomorrow I shall see the sun arise,
No ugly dream shall fright my mind, no ugly sight my eyes.

But slumber hold me tightly till I waken in the dawn,
And hear the thrushes singing in the lilacs round the lawn.

SYNOPSIS

The poem describes a day in the life of a happy boy.

ENRICHMENT ACTIVITIES

1. **Recite Poem Information**
   Recite the title of the poem and the name of the poet.
2. **Narrate the Poem**
   Narrate the poem events aloud using your own words.
3. **Study the Poem Picture**
   Study the poem picture and describe how it relates to the poem.
4. **Can You Find It?**
   Find the following in the poem picture: hair, shirt, shorts, and feet.

VOCABULARY

Recite and Copy Each Word	Recite the Definition
linen	Domestic textiles, such as tablecloths, bedding, towels, underclothes, etc., that are made of linen or linen-like fabric.
sleepsin-by	Sleep.
fright	A state of terror excited by the sudden appearance of danger.
slumber	A very light state of sleep, almost awake.
dawn	The morning twilight period immediately before sunrise.
thrush	Any of several species of songbirds, often with spotted underbellies.
lilacs	Large shrubs bearing white, pale pink, or purple flowers.

REVIEW QUESTIONS

1. What is the title of the poem?
2. What is the name of the poet who wrote "A Good Boy?"
3. What happens in the poem?
4. Where does the poem take place?
5. Who are the characters in the poem?
6. What does the poem teach the reader?

COLORING AND COPYWORK

I never said an ugly word,

but smiled and stuck to play.

LESSON 21. "WINDY NIGHTS" BY ROBERT LOUIS STEVENSON

FEATURED POEM (Children Practice Reciting the Poem with Instructor Assistance.)

1. Whenever the moon and stars are set,
Whenever the wind is high,
All night long in the dark and wet,
A man goes riding by.
Late in the night when the fires are out,
Why does he gallop and gallop about?

2. Whenever the trees are crying aloud,
And ships are tossed at sea,
By, on the highway, low and loud,
By at the gallop goes he.
By at the gallop he goes, and then
By he comes back at the gallop again.

SYNOPSIS

The poem describes a man galloping back and forth during the night.

ENRICHMENT ACTIVITIES

1. **Recite Poem Information**
   Recite the title of the poem and the name of the poet.
2. **Narrate the Poem**
   Narrate the poem events aloud using your own words.
3. **Study the Poem Picture**
   Study the poem picture and describe how it relates to the poem.
4. **Can You Find It?**
   Find the following in the poem picture: rider, reins, hooves, and tail.
5. **Discuss the Poem**
   The poem presents a mystery.
   - Why do you believe the man gallops about on windy nights?
   - Imagine a few scenarios. For example, perhaps he checks to ensure a nearby lighthouse is still lit to ensure the ships don't crash against the rocks.

VOCABULARY

Recite and Copy Each Word	Recite the Definition
gallop	The fastest gait of a horse, a two-beat stride during which all four legs are off the ground simultaneously.
tossed	To lift with a sudden or violent motion.

REVIEW QUESTIONS

1. What is the title of the poem?
2. What is the name of the poet who wrote "Windy Nights?"
3. What happens in the poem?
4. Who are the characters in the poem?
5. What does the poem teach the reader?

COLORING AND COPYWORK

All night long in the dark,

A man goes riding by.

LESSON 22. "THE SWING"
BY ROBERT LOUIS STEVENSON

FEATURED POEM (Children Practice Reciting the Poem with Instructor Assistance.)

How do you like to go up in a swing,
Up in the air so blue?
Oh, I do think it the pleasantest thing
Ever a child can do!

Up in the air and over the wall,
Till I can see so wide,
River and trees and cattle and all
Over the countryside--

Till I look down on the garden green,
Down on the roof so brown--
Up in the air I go flying again,
Up in the air and down!

SYNOPSIS

The poem describes the feelings and sights experienced when swinging through the air.

ENRICHMENT ACTIVITIES

1. **Recite Poem Information**
   Recite the title of the poem and the name of the poet.

2. **Narrate the Poem**
   Narrate the poem events aloud using your own words.

3. **Study the Poem Picture**
   Study the poem picture and describe how it relates to the poem.

4. **Can You Find It?**
   Find the following in the poem picture: swinging girl, pushing girl, girl picking flower, trunk, hat, grass, and bow in hair.

VOCABULARY

Recite and Copy Each Word	Recite the Definition
air	The substance constituting earth's atmosphere.
pleasantest (pleasant)	Pleasing in manner or nice.
cattle	Domesticated bovine animals such as cows, bulls, and steers.
countryside	A rural area.

REVIEW QUESTIONS

1. What is the title of the poem?
2. What is the name of the poet who wrote "The Swing?"
3. What happens in the poem?
4. Who are the characters in the poem?
5. What does the poem teach the reader?

COLORING AND COPYWORK

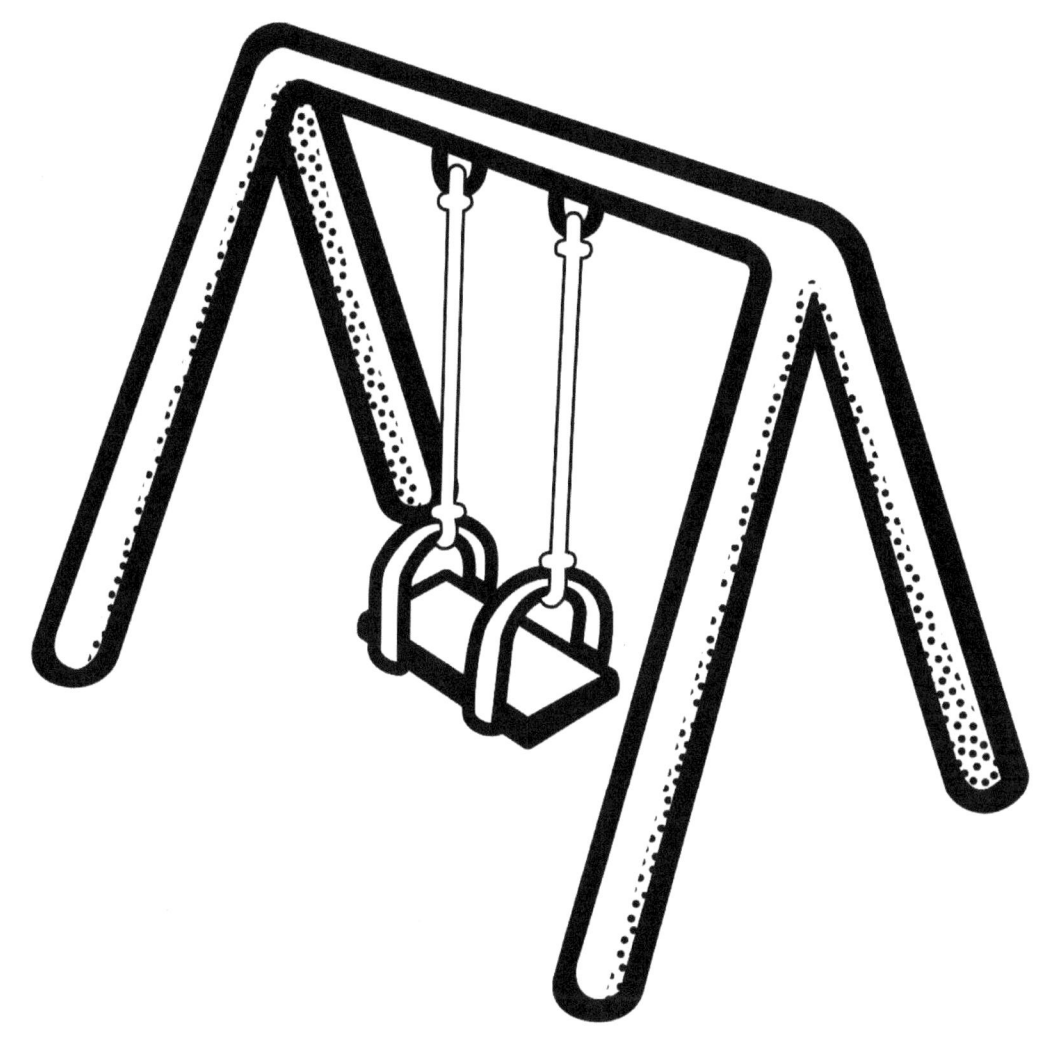

Up in the air I go flying again,

Up in the air and down

LESSON 23. "MY SHADOW" BY ROBERT LOUIS STEVENSON

FEATURED POEM (Children Practice Reciting the Poem with Instructor Assistance.)

I have a little shadow that goes in and out with me,
And what can be the use of him is more than I can see.
He is very, very like me from the heels up to the head;
And I see him jump before me, when I jump into my bed.

The funniest thing about him is the way he likes to grow--
Not at all like proper children, which is always very slow;
For he sometimes shoots up taller like an india-rubber ball,
And he sometimes gets so little that there's none of him at all.

He hasn't got a notion of how children ought to play,
And can only make a fool of me in every sort of way.
He stays so close behind me, he's a coward you can see;
I'd think shame to stick to nursie as that shadow sticks to me!

One morning, very early, before the sun was up,
I rose and found the shining dew on every buttercup;
But my lazy little shadow, like an arrant sleepy-head,
Had stayed at home behind me and was fast asleep in bed.

SYNOPSIS

The poem describes a child's observations of their shadow, which changes throughout the day and night.

ENRICHMENT ACTIVITIES

1. **Recite Poem Information**
   Recite the title of the poem and the name of the poet.

2. **Narrate the Poem**
   Narrate the poem events aloud using your own words.

3. **Study the Poem Picture**
   Study the poem picture and describe how it relates to the poem.

4. **Can You Find It?**
   Find the following in the poem picture: something pointing, shirt, pants, ear, and feet.

5. **Observe Your Shadow**
   - Go outside on a sunny day or stand between a bright light source and a wall.
   - Move about and watch your shadow.
   - Experiment by going outside at different times of day or moving your lamp. How does this change your shadow?

VOCABULARY

Recite and Copy Each Word	Recite the Definition
heel	The rear part of the foot, where it joins the leg.
proper	Suited or acceptable to the purpose or circumstances.
shoot	To move or act quickly or suddenly.
India-rubber	Natural rubber.
coward	A person who lacks courage.
arrant	Utter or complete (with a negative sense).

REVIEW QUESTIONS

1. What is the title of the poem?
2. What is the name of the poet who wrote "My Shadow?"
3. What happens in the poem?
4. Who are the characters in the poem?
5. What does the poem teach the reader?

COLORING AND COPYWORK

I have a little shadow that goes

in and out with me.

POET VI: ELLA WHEELER WILCOX
LESSON 24. "SOLITUDE"

POET OVERVIEW

- Ella Wheeler Wilcox was born in 1850 in Johnstown, Wisconsin.
- Wilcox infused her poems with passion, optimism, and joy. One of her most famous poems, "Solitude," contains the line, "Laugh, and the world laughs with you, Weep and you weep alone."
- After her marriage in 1884, Wilcox became very interested in the paranormal. She and her husband promised that whomever passed on first would communicate with the other from the spirit world.
- When her husband died after thirty years of marriage, Wilcox was distraught she received no message from beyond from her husband.
- Wilcox died of cancer at the age of 68 in Short Beach, Connecticut.

COLOR THE POET

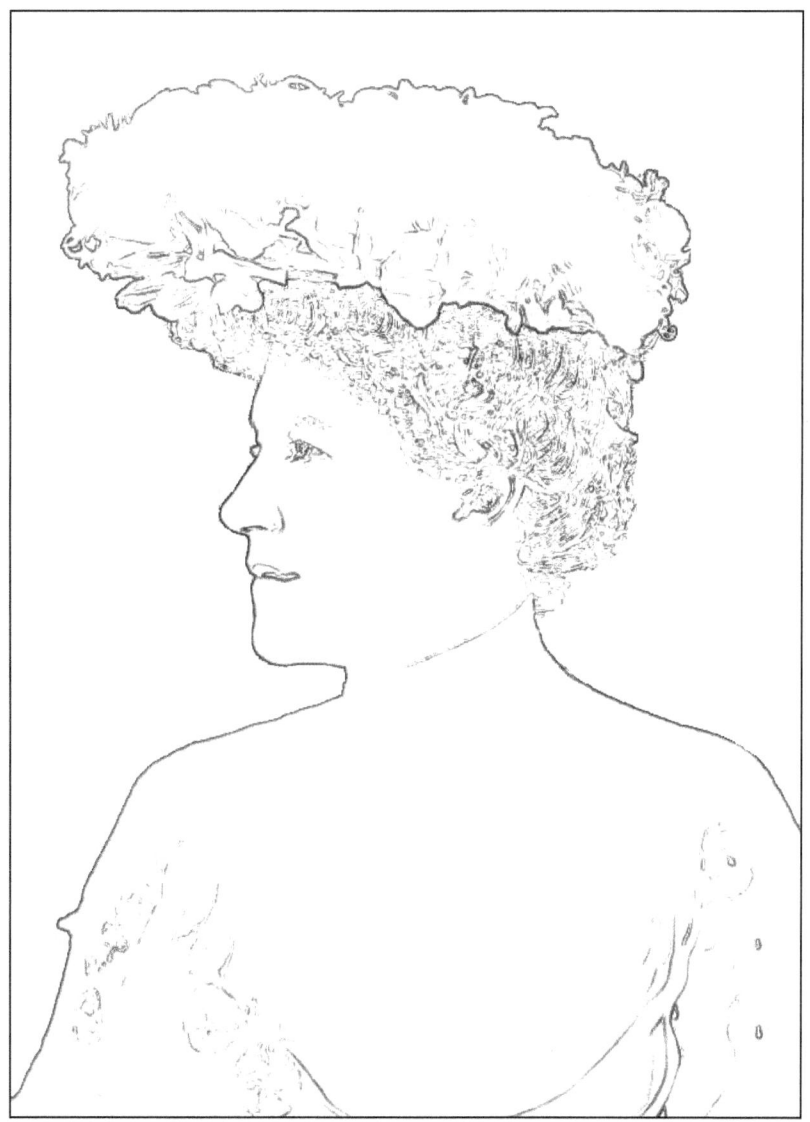

MAP THE POET

Locate and color Wilcox's state of birth, **Wisconsin (WI)**, and state of death, **Connecticut (CT)**, on the map of the United States.

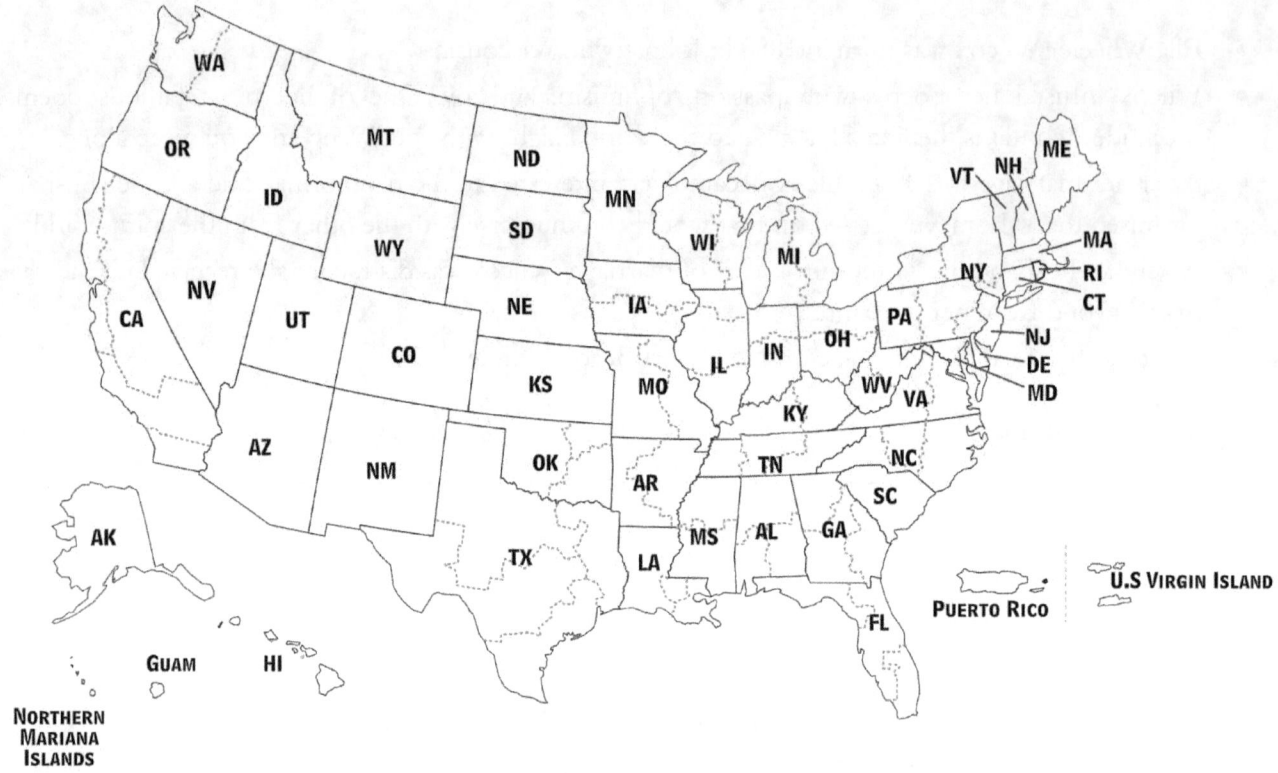

FEATURED POEM (Children Practice Reciting the Poem with Instructor Assistance.)

1. Laugh, and the world laughs with you;

Weep, and you weep alone.

For the sad old earth must borrow its mirth,

But has trouble enough of its own.

Sing, and the hills will answer;

Sigh, it is lost on the air.

The echoes bound to a joyful sound,

But shrink from voicing care.

2. Rejoice, and men will seek you;

Grieve, and they turn and go.

They want full measure of all your pleasure,

But they do not need your woe.

Be glad, and your friends are many;

Be sad, and you lose them all.

There are none to decline your nectared wine,

But alone you must drink life's gall.

3. Feast, and your halls are crowded;

Fast, and the world goes by.

Succeed and give, and it helps you live,

But no man can help you die.

There is room in the halls of pleasure

For a long and lordly train,

But one by one we must all file on

Through the narrow aisles of pain.

SYNOPSIS

The poem states people gravitate to those who are happy and shun those who are sad.

ENRICHMENT ACTIVITIES

1. **Recite Poem Information**
   Recite the title of the poem and the name of the poet.

2. **Narrate the Poem**
   Narrate the poem events aloud using your own words.

3. **Study the Poem Pictures**
   Study the poem pictures and describe how they relate to the poem.

4. **Can You Find It?**
   Find the following in the poem pictures: sad woman, happy woman, and solemn man.

5. **Discuss Fair-Weather Friends**
   - This poem describes people who are fair-weather friends. Fair-weather friends are those who are friendly, helpful, or available only when it is advantageous or convenient to be so.
   - True friends are those who also support you when you are sad or having trouble.
   - Name any people in your life who are true friends. This might include close family members or friends.
   - List some ways you can be a true friend to your loved ones.

VOCABULARY

Recite and Copy Each Word	Recite the Definition
solitude	State of being alone or solitary.
weep	To cry.
mirth	The emotion usually following humor and accompanied by laughter.
echoes	A reflected sound that is heard again by its initial observer.
rejoice	To be very happy or delighted.
grieve	To feel very sad about or to mourn.
nectared	Filled with nectar, a sweet and sugary solution.
feast	A very large meal, often of a ceremonial nature.
fast	To restrict one's personal consumption, generally of food, commonly for religious or medical reasons.

REVIEW QUESTIONS

1. What is the title of the poem?
2. What is the name of the poet who wrote "Solitude?"
3. What happens in the poem?
4. Who are the characters in the poem?
5. What does the poem teach the reader?

COLORING AND COPYWORK

Laugh, and the world laughs

Weep, and you weep alone.

LESSON 25. "A FABLE"
BY ELLA WHEELER WILCOX

FEATURED POEM (Children Practice Reciting the Poem with Instructor Assistance.)

1. Some cawing Crows, a hooting Owl,
A Hawk, a Canary, an old Marsh-Fowl,
One day all meet together
To hold a caucus and settle the fate
Of a certain bird (without a mate),
A bird of another feather.

2. "My friends," said the Owl, with a look most wise,
"The Eagle is soaring too near the skies,
In a way that is quite improper;
Yet the world is praising her, so I'm told,
And I think her actions have grown so bold
That some of us ought to stop her."

3. "I have heard it said," quoth Hawk, with a sigh,
"That young lambs died at the glance of her eye,
And I wholly scorn and despise her.
This, and more, I am told they say,
And I think that the only proper way
Is never to recognize her."

4. "I am quite convinced," said Crow, with a caw,
"That the Eagle minds no moral law,
She's a most unruly creature."
"She's an ugly thing," piped Canary Bird;
"Some call her handsome—it's so absurd—

5. She hasn't a decent feature."
Then the old Marsh-Hen went hopping about,
She said she was sure—she hadn't a doubt—
Of the truth of each bird's story:
And she thought it a duty to stop her flight,
To pull her down from her lofty height,
And take the gilt from her glory.

6. But, lo! from a peak on the mountain grand
That looks out over the smiling land
And over the mighty ocean,
The Eagle is spreading her splendid wings—
She rises, rises, and upward swings,
With a slow, majestic motion.

7. Up in the blue of God's own skies,
With a cry of rapture, away she flies,
Close to the Great Eternal:
She sweeps the world with her piercing sight;
Her soul is filled with the infinite
And the joy of things supernal.

8. Thus rise forever the chosen of God,
The genius-crowned or the power-shod,
Over the dust-world sailing;
And back, like splinters blown by the winds,
Must fall the missiles of silly minds,
Useless and unavailing.

SYNOPSIS

A group of birds discusses reprimanding an eagle that they feel soars too high in the sky. The eagle ignores their gossiping and continues to soar through the sky.

ENRICHMENT ACTIVITIES

1. **Recite Poem Information**
   Recite the title of the poem and the name of the poet.
2. **Narrate the Poem**
   Narrate the poem events aloud using your own words.
3. **Study the Poem Picture**
   Study the poem picture and describe how it relates to the poem.
4. **Can You Find It?**
   Find the following in the poem picture: wings, tail feathers, and feet.
5. **Discuss Gossip**
   - Describe the subject of the birds' gossip.
   - Do you think it is right for the birds to gossip? Why or why not?
   - Do you think gossiping is bullying behavior? Why or why not?
   - What is the eagle's strategy of dealing with the gossip?
   - Do you think her strategy will be effective? Why or why not?

VOCABULARY

Recite and Copy Each Word	Recite the Definition
caucus	A meeting.
settle	To determine a resolution to something in doubt or question.
unruly	Wild or uncontrolled.
lofty	High, tall, or having great height or stature.
gilt	Adorned by gold or other metal in a thin layer.

Recite and Copy Each Word	Recite the Definition
supernal	Pertaining to heaven or to the sky.
unavailing	Fruitless, futile, or useless.
gossip	Idle talk about someone's private or personal matters, especially someone not present.

REVIEW QUESTIONS

1. What is the title of the poem?
2. What is the name of the poet who wrote "A Fable?"
3. What happens in the poem?
4. Who are the characters in the poem?
5. What does the poem teach the reader?

COLORING AND COPYWORK

Her soul fills with the infinite

And the joy of things supernal.

Color the following birds and recite their names:

LESSON 26. "SUNSET"
BY ELLA WHEELER WILCOX

FEATURED POEM (Children Practice Reciting the Poem with Instructor Assistance.)

I saw the day lean o'er the world's sharp edge

And peer into night's chasm, dark and damp;

High in his hand he held a blazing lamp,

Then dropped it and plunged headlong down the ledge.

With lurid splendor that swift paled to gray,

I saw the dim skies suddenly flush bright.

'Twas but the expiring glory of the light

Flung from the hand of the adventurous day.

SYNOPSIS

The poem personifies "day" (writes as if "day" is a person). Day lowers a lamp (the sun) over the edge of the world (the horizon) at sunset.

ENRICHMENT ACTIVITIES

1. **Recite Poem Information**
   Recite the title of the poem and the name of the poet.

2. **Narrate the Poem**
   Narrate the poem events aloud using your own words.

3. **Study the Poem Picture**
   Study the poem picture and describe how it relates to the poem.

4. **Can You Find It?**
   Find the following in the poem picture: carrying handle, glass, metal base, chimney (very top), flame, and wick raiser knob.

VOCABULARY

Recite and Copy Each Word	Recite the Definition
edge	A sharp terminating border.
chasm	A deep, steep-sided rift, gap, or fissure.
blazing	Burning with a fire producing a lot of flames and light.
plunged	Dove, leaped, or rushed.
headlong	Rashly or in haste.
lurid	Being of a light-yellow hue.
swift	Fast or rapid.
expiring	Dying or ending.
flung	Thrown violently or carelessly.

REVIEW QUESTIONS

1. What is the title of the poem?
2. What is the name of the poet who wrote "Sunset?"
3. What happens in the poem?
4. Who are the characters in the poem?
5. What does the poem teach the reader?

COLORING AND COPYWORK

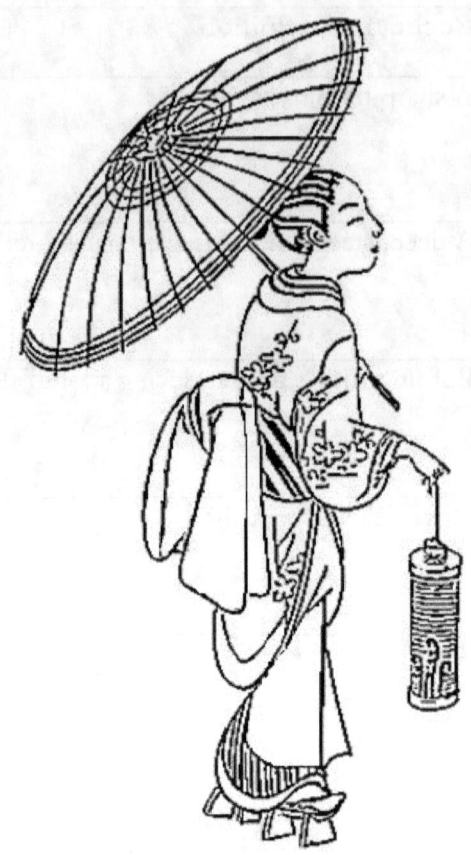

High in her hand

Day held a blazing lamp.

LESSON 27. "A MARCH SNOW"
BY ELLA WHEELER WILCOX

FEATURED POEM (Children Practice Reciting the Poem with Instructor Assistance.)

Let the old snow be covered with the new:
The trampled snow, so soiled, and stained, and sodden.
Let it be hidden wholly from our view
By pure white flakes, all trackless and untrodden.
When Winter dies, low at the sweet Spring's feet
Let him be mantled in a clean, white sheet.

Let the old life be covered by the new:
The old past life so full of sad mistakes,
Let it be wholly hidden from the view
By deeds as white and silent as snow-flakes.

Ere this earth life melts in the eternal Spring
Let the white mantle of repentance fling
Soft drapery about it, fold on fold,
Even as the new snow covers up the old.

SYNOPSIS

The narrator asks that the dirty March snow be covered in a white sheet of new snow. The narrator asks that their own mistakes be similarly covered in a white sheet of repentance.

ENRICHMENT ACTIVITIES

1. **Recite Poem Information**
   Recite the title of the poem and the name of the poet.

2. **Narrate the Poem**
   Narrate the poem events aloud using your own words.

3. **Study the Poem Picture**
   Study the poem picture and describe how it relates to the poem.

4. **Discuss the Poem**
   - The poem compares a white sheet of new snow to a white sheet of repentance covering our past mistakes.
   - Think about a mistake you once made.
   - Everyone makes mistakes, but how you react to your mistakes can define you as a person.
   - What can we do when we make mistakes?
     - We can express sincere regret and apologize when we've inconvenienced or hurt someone.
     - We can take action to right the mistake we made.
     - We can avoid repeating the mistake again.

VOCABULARY

Recite and Copy Each Word	Recite the Definition
trampled	Crushed something by walking on it.
soiled	Dirtied.
untrodden	Never walked upon, unspoiled, or unexplored.
mantle	A piece of clothing somewhat like an open robe or cloak.
repentance	A feeling of regret or remorse for doing wrong.
drapery	Cloth draped gracefully in folds.

REVIEW QUESTIONS

1. What is the title of the poem?
2. What is the name of the poet who wrote "A March Snow?"
3. What happens in the poem?
4. Who are the characters in the poem?
5. What does the poem teach the reader?

ELEMENTARY POETRY VOLUME 3: POETRY OF NATURE, REVELRY, AND RHYME

COLORING AND COPYWORK

Soft drapery, fold on fold,

The new snow covers up the old.

POET I: ABBIE FARWELL BROWN
LESSON 28. "THE FISHERMAN"

POET OVERVIEW

- Abbie Farwell Brown was born in 1871 in Boston, Massachusetts.
- Brown founded her high school newspaper, "The Jabberwock," one of the oldest newspapers in the United States.
- Brown published children's books, children's poetry, and adult poetry.
- Brown also helped to write "On the Trail," the official song of the USA Girl Scouts.
- Brown died of cancer at the age of 55 in Boston, Massachusetts.

MAP THE POET

Locate and color Brown's state of birth, **Massachusetts (MA)**, on the map of the United States.

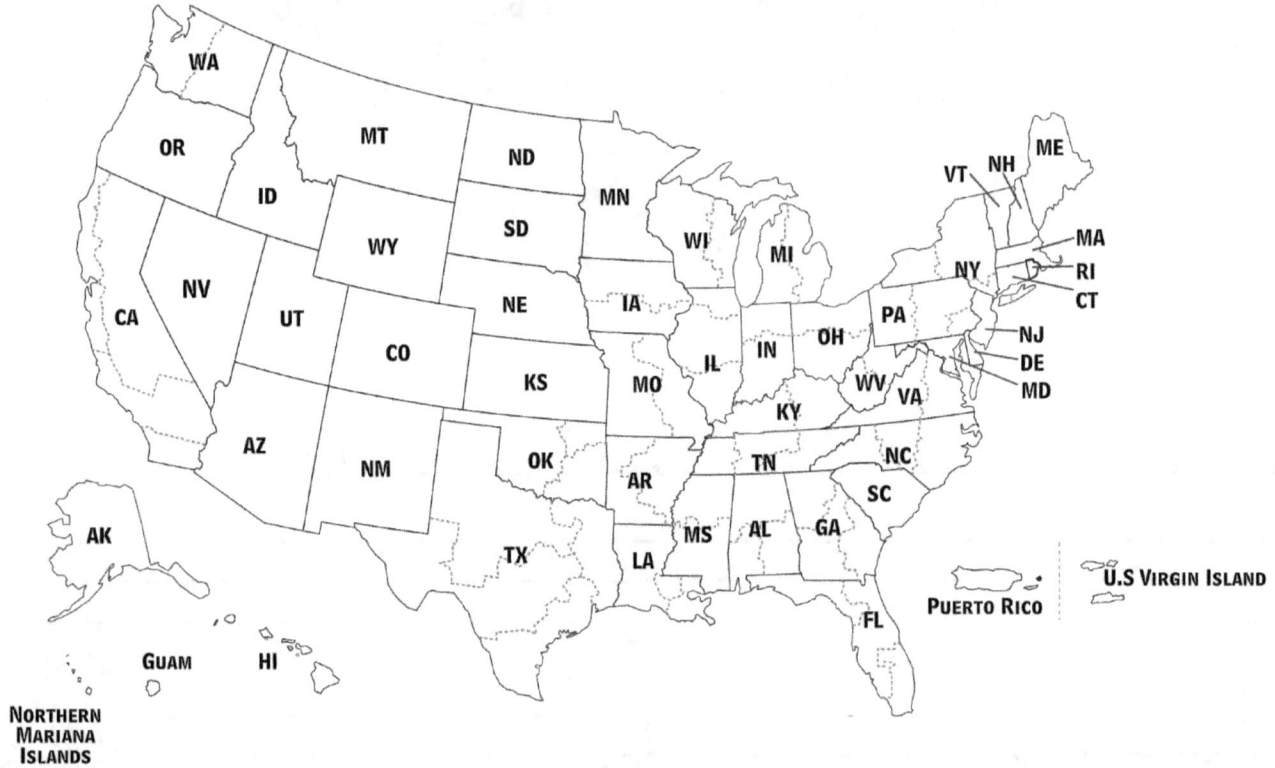

FEATURED POEM (Children Practice Reciting the Poem with Instructor Assistance.)

1. The fisherman goes out at dawn
When everyone's abed,
And from the bottom of the sea
Draws up his daily bread.

2. His life is strange; half on the shore
And half upon the sea –
Not quite a fish, and yet not quite
The same as you and me.

3. The fisherman has curious eyes;
They make you feel so queer,
As if they had seen many things
Of wonder and of fear.

4. They're like the sea on foggy days, --
Not gray, nor yet quite blue;
They're like the wondrous tales he tells
Not quite -- yet maybe -- true.

5. He knows so much of boats and tides,
Of winds and clouds and sky!
But when I tell of city things,
He sniffs and shuts one eye!

SYNOPSIS

The poem describes a fisherman with curious eyes who lives half upon the shore and half upon the sea.

ENRICHMENT ACTIVITIES

1. **Recite Poem Information**
   Recite the title of the poem and the name of the poet.

2. **Narrate the Poem**
   Narrate the poem events aloud using your own words.

3. **Study the Poem Picture**
   Study the poem picture and describe how it relates to the poem.

4. **Can You Find It?**
   Find the following in the poem picture: fishing boat, fishing pole, fishing line, water, and fisherman.

VOCABULARY

Recite and Copy Each Word	Recite the Definition
dawn	The morning twilight period immediately before sunrise.
abed	In bed.
wondrous	Amazing, inspiring awe, or marvelous.

REVIEW QUESTIONS

1. What is the title of the poem?
2. What is the name of the poet who wrote "The Fisherman?"
3. What happens in the poem?
4. Who are the characters in the poem?
5. What does a fisherman do for a living?
6. How is the fisherman described in the poem different from many other people?

COLORING AND COPYWORK

The fisherman goes out at dawn

When everyone's abed.

LESSON 29. "FRIENDS" BY ABBIE FARWELL BROWN

FEATURED POEM (Children Practice Reciting the Poem with Instructor Assistance.)

1. How good to lie a little while
And look up through the tree!
The Sky is like a kind big smile
Bent sweetly over me.

2. The Sunshine flickers through the lace
Of leaves above my head,
And kisses me upon the face
Like Mother, before bed.

3. The Wind comes stealing o'er the grass
To whisper pretty things;
And though I cannot see him pass,
I feel his careful wings.

4. So many gentle Friends are near
Whom one can scarcely see,
A child should never feel a fear,
Wherever he may be.

SYNOPSIS

The narrator describes their Friends – the Sky, the Sunshine, and the Wind.

ENRICHMENT ACTIVITIES

1. **Recite Poem Information**
   Recite the title of the poem and the name of the poet.

2. **Narrate the Poem**
   Narrate the poem events aloud using your own words.

3. **Study the Poem Picture**
   Study the poem picture and describe how it relates to the poem.

4. **Can You Find It?**

   Find the following in the poem picture: child, flowers, butterflies, grass, tree, and friends.

5. **Discuss the Poem**
   - The poem narrator describes her non-human friends, including the wind and the sunshine.
   - Discuss whether you think humans can have non-human friends.
   - If you agree that humans can have non-human friends, provide some examples.

VOCABULARY

Recite and Copy Each Word	Recite the Definition
friend	A person other than a family member, spouse, or romantic partner whose company one enjoys and towards whom one feels affection.
lace	A light fabric containing patterns of holes, usually built up from a single thread.
scarcely	Barely or hardly.

REVIEW QUESTIONS

1. What is the title of the poem?
2. What is the name of the poet who wrote "Friends?"
3. What happens in the poem?
4. Who are the characters in the poem?
5. Do you believe the Sky, the Sunshine, and the Wind can truly be our friends? What about animals? Why or why not?

COLORING AND COPYWORK

Sunshine flickers through the lace

Of leaves above my head.

LESSON 30. "THE FAITHLESS FLOWERS"
BY ABBIE FARWELL BROWN

FEATURED POEM (Children Practice Reciting the Poem with Instructor Assistance.)

I went this morning down to where the Johnny-Jump-Ups grow
Like naughty purple faces nodding in a row.
I stayed 'most all the morning there –
I sat down on a stump and watched and watched them –
And they never gave a jump!

And Golden-Glow that stands up tall and yellow by the fence,
It doesn't glow a single bit –
Its only just pretense –
I ran down after tea last night to watch them in the dark-
I had to light a match to see;
They didn't give a spark!

And then the Bouncing Bets don't bounce –
I tried them yesterday,
I picked a big bunch down in the meadow where they stay,
I took a piece of string I had and tied them in a ball,
And threw them down as hard has hard-
They never bounced at all!

And tiger-lilies may look fierce,
To meet the all alone,
All tall and black and yellowy and nodding like a stone
But they're no more like tigers than dogwood's a dog,
Or bulrushes are like a bull or toadwort like a frog!

I like the flowers very much – they're pleasant as can be
For bunches on the table, and to pick and wear and see,
But still it doesn't seem quite fair –
It does seem very queer
They don't do what they're named for –
Not at any time of year!

SYNOPSIS

The narrator wonders why flowers don't live up to their names. Johnny-Jump-Ups don't jump. Golden-Glows don't glow. Bouncing Bets don't bounce. Tiger lilies aren't fierce like tigers. Dogwoods aren't like dogs. Bulrushes aren't like bulls. Toadworts aren't like frogs.

ENRICHMENT ACTIVITIES

1. **Recite Poem Information**
   Recite the title of the poem and the name of the poet.
2. **Narrate the Poem**
   Narrate the poem events aloud using your own words.
3. **Study the Poem Picture**
   Study the poem picture (frame) and describe how it relates to the poem.
4. **Can You Find It?**
   Find the following in the poem picture: lilies, ribbons, and leaves.

VOCABULARY

Recite and Copy Each Word	Recite the Definition
faithless	Serving to disappoint or deceive.
pretense	An unsupported claim made or implied.
fierce	Exceedingly violent, severe, ferocious, or savage.
bunch	A group of similar things.

REVIEW QUESTIONS

1. What is the title of the poem?
2. What is the name of the poet who wrote "The Faithless Flowers?"
3. What happens in the poem?
4. Who are the characters in the poem?

COLORING AND COPYWORK

I like the flowers very much,

they're pleasant as can be.

LESSON 31. "BABY'S VALENTINE" BY ABBIE FARWELL BROWN

FEATURED POEM (Children Practice Reciting the Poem with Instructor Assistance.)

Valentine, O Valentine,

Pretty little Love of mine;

Little Love whose yellow hair

Makes the daffodils despair

Little Love whose shining eyes

Fill the stars with sad surprise

Hither turn your ten wee toes,

Each a tiny shut-up rose,

End most fitting and complete

For the rosy-pinky feet;

Toddle, toddle here to me,

For I'm waiting, don't you see?

Waiting for to call you mine,

Valentine, O Valentine! Valentine, O Valentine!

I will dress you up so fine,

Here's a frock of tulip-leaves,

Trimmed with lace the spider weaves;

Here's a cap of larkspur blue,

Just precisely made for you;

Here's a mantle scarlet-dyed,

Once the tiger-lily's pride,

Spotted all with velvet black

Like the fire-beetle's back;

Lady-slippers on your feet,

Now behold you all complete!

Come and let me call you mine,

Valentine, O Valentine! Valentine, O Valentine!

Now a wreath for you I'll twine.

I will set you on a throne

Where the damask rose has blown,

Dropping all her velvet bloom,

Carpeting your leafy room:

Here while you shall sit in pride,

Butterflies all rainbow-pied,

Dandy beetles gold and green,

Creeping, flying, shall be seen

Every bird that shakes his wings,

Every katydid that sings

Wasp and bee with buzz and hum.

Hither, hither see them come,

Creeping all before your feet,

Rendering their homage meet.

But 'tis I call you mine, Valentine, O Valentine!

SYNOPSIS

The narrator describes their love and adoration for a baby. The narrator promises to clothe the baby in beautiful flowers and set the baby on a flower throne. The narrator says bugs will worship the baby. It is unclear whether the ode is to a human baby or perhaps a fairy baby.

ENRICHMENT ACTIVITIES

1. **Recite Poem Information**
   Recite the title of the poem and the name of the poet.

2. **Narrate the Poem**
   Narrate the poem events aloud using your own words.

3. **Study the Poem Pictures**
   Study the poem pictures and describe how they relate to the poem.

4. **Can You Find It?**
   Find the following in the poem pictures: woman, baby, Valentine, rose, petals, and leaves.

VOCABULARY

Recite and Copy Each Word	Recite the Definition
valentine	1. An expression of affection, usually in the form of greeting card or gift, given the object of one's affection, especially on February 14th. 2. A person to whom a valentine is given or from whom it is received.
hither	To this place, to here.
toddle	To walk unsteadily, as a small child does.
frock	A dress.
twine	The act of winding round.
pied	Decorated or colored in blotches.
dandy	Excellent or first-rate.
homage	A demonstration of respect, such as toward an individual.

REVIEW QUESTIONS

1. What is the title of the poem?
2. What is the name of the poet who wrote "Baby's Valentine?"
3. What happens in the poem?
4. Who are the characters in the poem?

COLORING AND COPYWORK

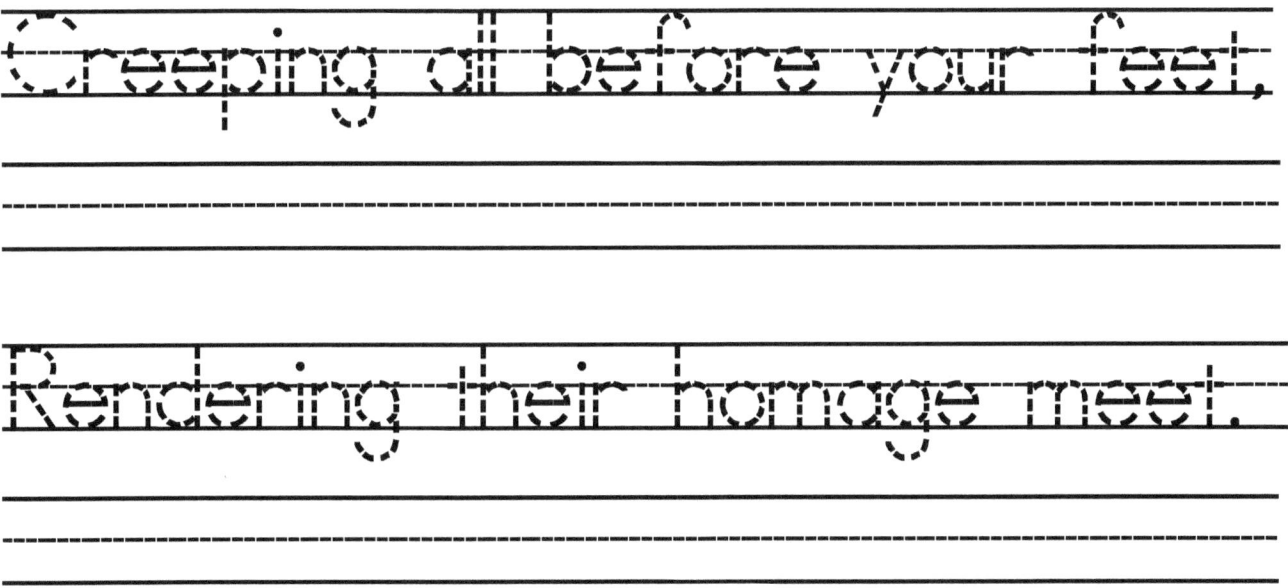

SONJA GLUMICH

LESSON 32. "A TRYST" BY ABBIE FARWELL BROWN

FEATURED POEM (Children Practice Reciting the Poem with Instructor Assistance.)

A tryst had I with the bright sun to keep

Upon a little hill-top in the dew;

I promised him to wake mine eyes from sleep

And see him paint the dappled dawn anew,

To meet him by the rose-bush in the brake,

Aye, even before the lark should be awake.

I gave my promise as the sun sank red,

And then I softly stole away to bed.

SYNOPSIS

The narrator promises to meet the sun at dawn the following day, watches the sun set, and goes to bed.

ENRICHMENT ACTIVITIES

1. **Recite Poem Information**
   Recite the title of the poem and the name of the poet.

2. **Narrate the Poem**
   Narrate the poem events aloud using your own words.

3. **Study the Poem Picture**
   Study the poem picture and describe how it relates to the poem.

4. **Can You Find It?**
   Find the following in the poem picture: sun, eyes, eyelashes, lips, nose, and rays.

VOCABULARY

Recite and Copy Each Word	Recite the Definition
tryst	A prearranged meeting or assignation.
dew	Moisture in the air that settles on plants or other items in the morning, resulting in drops.
dappled	Marked with mottling or spots.
anew	Again or once more.
brake	A thicket, or an area overgrown with briers.
aye	Yes; a word expressing assent or an affirmative answer to a question.
lark	Any of various small, singing birds.

REVIEW QUESTIONS

1. What is the title of the poem?
2. What is the name of the poet who wrote "A Tryst?"
3. What happens in the poem?
4. Who are the characters in the poem?

COLORING AND COPYWORK

A tryst had I with the sun to keep

Upon a little hill-top in the dew.

POET VIII: SARA TEASDALE
LESSON 33. "THERE WILL COME SOFT RAINS"

POET OVERVIEW

- Sara Trevor Teasdale was born in 1884 in St. Louis, Missouri.

- Teasdale had two older brothers and an older sister.

- Teasdale's first spoken word was, "pretty." Her mother suggested that this love of pretty things inspired Teasdale to write poetry.

- Teasdale eventually married, but the marriage ended in divorce after fifteen years. After her divorce, she devoted herself to her poetry.

- Teasdale was frail and sickly for most of her life. After suffering from chronic pneumonia, Teasdale died at the age of 48 in New York City, New York.

COLOR THE POET

MAP THE POET

Locate and color Teasdale's state of birth, **Missouri (MO)**, and place of death, **New York (NY)**, on the map of the United States.

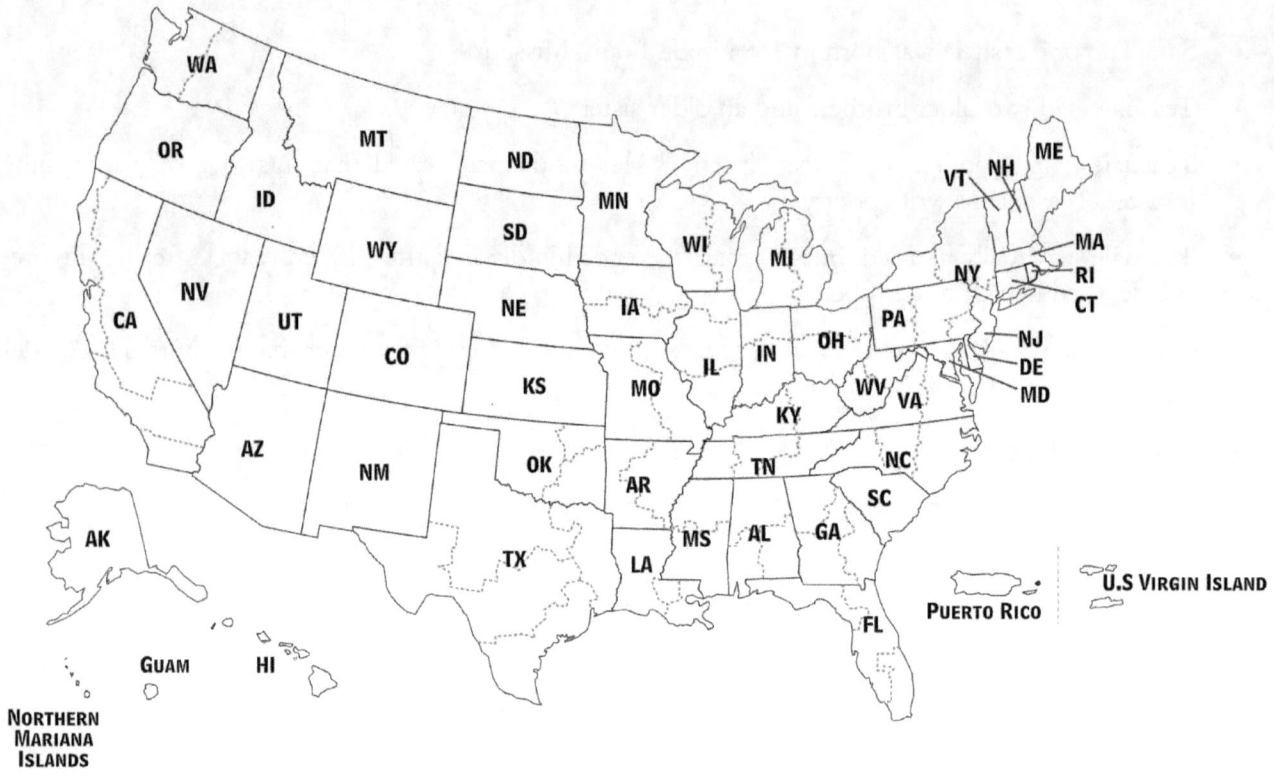

FEATURED POEM (Children Practice Reciting the Poem with Instructor Assistance.)

There will come soft rains and the smell of the ground,
And swallows circling in their shimmering sound;
And frogs in the pools singing at night,
And wild plum trees in tremulous white;

Robins will wear their feathery fire,
Whistling their whims on a low fence-wire;
And not one will know of the war, not one
Will care at last when it is done.

Not one would mind, neither bird nor tree,
If mankind perished utterly;
And Spring herself, when she woke at dawn
Would scarcely know that we were gone.

SYNOPSIS

The poem questions the importance of humankind to the rain, the animals, the plants, and the passing seasons.

ENRICHMENT ACTIVITIES

1. **Recite Poem Information**
   Recite the title of the poem and the name of the poet.
2. **Narrate the Poem**
   Narrate the poem events aloud using your own words.
3. **Study the Poem Picture**
   Study the poem picture and describe how it relates to the poem.
4. **Can You Find It?**
   Find the following in the poem picture: cloud, droplets, and something falling.
5. **Discuss the Poem**
   - Imagine all humans leaving the earth in big spaceships.
   - Do you think the remaining plants and animals would thrive, wither, or remain largely unchanged without humans on earth?

VOCABULARY

Recite and Copy Each Word	Recite the Definition
tremulous	Trembling, quivering, or shaking.
whims	Fanciful impulses or whimsical ideas.
perished	Died or disappeared.
utterly	Completely or entirely.
scarcely	Barely, hardly, or almost not at all.

REVIEW QUESTIONS

1. What is the title of the poem?
2. What is the name of the poet who wrote "There Will Come Soft Rains?"
3. What happens in the poem?
4. Who are the characters in the poem?
5. Which scents does the poem incorporate?
6. Which sounds does the poem describe?

COLORING AND COPYWORK

There will come soft rains.

LESSON 34. "BARTER"
BY SARA TEASDALE

FEATURED POEM (Children Practice Reciting the Poem with Instructor Assistance.)

Life has loveliness to sell,
All beautiful and splendid things,
Blue waves whitened on a cliff,
Soaring fire that sways and sings,
And children's faces looking up
Holding wonder like a cup.

Life has loveliness to sell,
Music like a curve of gold,
Scent of pine trees in the rain,
Eyes that love you, arms that hold,
And for your spirit's still delight,
Holy thoughts that star the night.

Spend all you have for loveliness,
Buy it and never count the cost;
For one white singing hour of peace
Count many a year of strife well lost,
And for a breath of ecstasy
Give all you have been, or could be.

SYNOPSIS

The poem advises us to spend all we have on the loveliness and peace sold by life.

ENRICHMENT ACTIVITIES

1. **Recite Poem Information**
   Recite the title of the poem and the name of the poet.

2. **Narrate the Poem**
   Narrate the poem events aloud using your own words.

3. **Study the Poem Picture**
   Study the poem picture and describe how it relates to the poem.

4. **Can You Find It?**
   Find the following in the poem picture: lady, leaves, trees, trunks, wavy hair, and draped dress.

VOCABULARY

Recite and Copy Each Word	Recite the Definition
barter	An exchange of goods or services without the use of money.
loveliness	The property of being lovely, attractive, or lovable.
strife	Conflict, sometimes violent, usually brief or limited in scope.
ecstasy	A feeling of great joy or happiness.

REVIEW QUESTIONS

1. What is the title of the poem?
2. What is the name of the poet who wrote "Barter?"
3. What happens in the poem?
4. Who are the characters in the poem?
5. The title of the poem is "Barter." What must we give to life in exchange for the things life has to sell?
6. What does life have to sell?

COLORING AND COPYWORK

And children's faces looking up

Holding wonder like a cup.

LESSON 35. "LET IT BE FORGOTTEN" BY SARA TEASDALE

FEATURED POEM (Children Practice Reciting the Poem with Instructor Assistance.)

Let it be forgotten, as a flower is forgotten,
Forgotten as a fire that once was singing gold,
Let it be forgotten forever and ever,
Time is a kind friend, he will make us old.

If anyone asks, say it was forgotten
Long and long ago,
As a flower, as a fire, as a hushed footfall
In a long forgotten snow.

SYNOPSIS

The poem asks that something be forgotten like faded flowers, extinguished fires, or the past sound of a footstep in long ago melted snow.

ENRICHMENT ACTIVITIES

1. **Recite Poem Information**
   Recite the title of the poem and the name of the poet.

2. **Narrate the Poem**
   Narrate the poem events aloud using your own words.

3. **Study the Poem Picture**
   Study the poem picture and describe how it relates to the poem.

4. **Discuss the Poem**
   - Describe something embarrassing that happened to you.
   - If one thing from your life could be forgotten by everyone else, what would it be?
   - If you had the power to forget anything yourself, what would you forget?

VOCABULARY

Recite and Copy Each Word	Recite the Definition
forgotten	Of which knowledge has been lost or which is no longer remembered.
hushed	Quieted.
footfall	The sound made by a footstep.

REVIEW QUESTIONS

1. What is the title of the poem?
2. What is the name of the poet who wrote "Let It Be Forgotten?"
3. What happens in the poem?
4. Who are the characters in the poem?
5. What was once "singing gold" in the poem?

COLORING AND COPYWORK

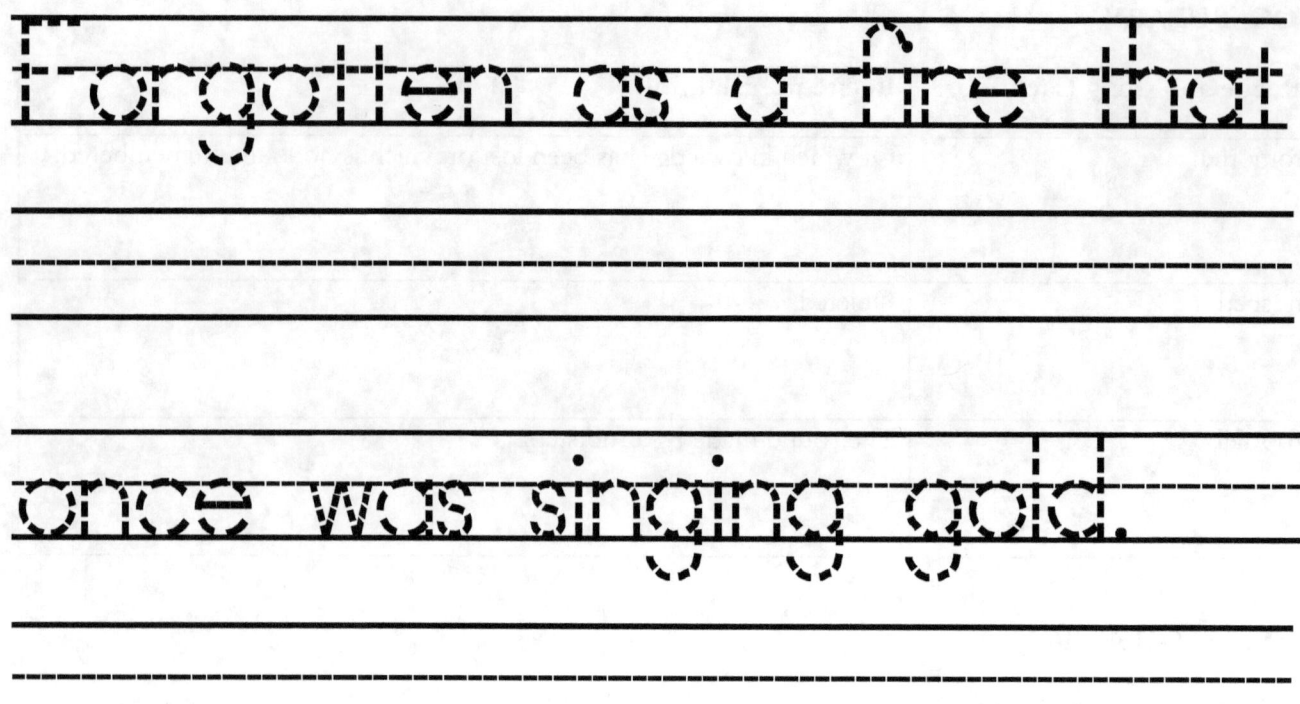

Forgotten as a fire that once was singing gold.

ELEMENTARY POETRY VOLUME 3: POETRY OF NATURE, REVELRY, AND RHYME

LESSON 36. "WISHES"
BY SARA TEASDALE

FEATURED POEM (Children Practice Reciting the Poem with Instructor Assistance.)

1. I wish for such a lot of things
That never will come true —
And yet I want them all so much
I think they might, don't you?

2. I want a little kitty-cat
That's soft and tame and sweet,
And every day I watch and hope
I'll find one in the street.

3. But nursie says, "Come, walk along,
"Don't stand and stare like that" —
I'm only looking hard and hard
To try to find my cat.

4. And then I want a blue balloon
That tries to fly away,
I thought if I wished hard enough
That it would come someday.

5. One time when I was in the park
I knew that it would be
Beside the big old clock at home
A-waiting there for me —

6. And soon as we got home again,
I hurried thro' the hall,
And looked beside the big old clock —
It wasn't there at all.

7. I think I'll never wish again —
But then, what shall I do?
The wishes are a lot of fun
Altho' they don't come true.

SYNOPSIS

The child narrator enjoys wishing for a kitty and a blue balloon, despite knowing the wishes will likely never come true.

ENRICHMENT ACTIVITIES

1. **Recite Poem Information**
   Recite the title of the poem and the name of the poet.
2. **Narrate the Poem**
   Narrate the poem events aloud using your own words.

3. **Study the Poem Picture**

    Study the poem picture and describe how it relates to the poem.

4. **Can You Find It?**

    Find the following in the poem pictures: whiskers, paw, balloon, string, and reflected light.

5. **Discuss Your Wishes**

    - In the poem, the child narrator enjoys wishing for things they will probably never get.
    - List some things you wish for the most.
    - Do you think you will get the things you wish for? Discuss why or why not.

VOCABULARY

Recite and Copy Each Word	Recite the Definition
wish	A desire, hope, or longing for something or for something to happen.
tame	Mild, well-behaved, and accustomed to human contact.
nursie	Nurse.

REVIEW QUESTIONS

1. What is the title of the poem?
2. What is the name of the poet who wrote "Wishes?"
3. What happens in the poem?
4. Who are the characters in the poem?
5. Do you think it is worthwhile to wish for things that will likely never come true?

COLORING AND COPYWORK

I want a little kitty-cat

That's soft and tame and sweet.

ANSWERS TO REVIEW QUESTIONS

LESSON 1
1. **What is the title of the poem?** The title of the poem is "The Crocodile."
2. **What is the name of the poet who wrote "The Crocodile?"** The name of the poet is Lewis Carroll.
3. **What happens in the poem?** A crocodile swims in the Nile River and eats little fishes.
4. **Where does the poem take place?** The poem takes place in the waters of the Nile river in Africa.
5. **List the animal characters in the poem.** The animal characters are a crocodile and little fishes.

LESSON 2
1. **What is the title of the poem?** The title of the poem is "The Walrus and The Carpenter."
2. **What is the name of the poet who wrote "The Walrus and The Carpenter?"** The name of the poet is Lewis Carroll.
3. **What happens in the poem?** The Walrus and the Carpenter invite the Oysters to walk with them on the beach. The eldest Oyster refuses, but many other Oysters agree. The Carpenter and Walrus take the oysters for a walk and then eat them.
4. **Where does the poem take place?** The poem takes place on a beach in the middle of the night.
5. **Who are the characters in the poem?** The characters in the poem are the Walrus, the Carpenter, and the Oysters.
6. **Why is the moon mad at the sun?** The moon is upset that the sun is shining in the middle of the night.
7. **Why do the oysters worry about being eaten when the Walrus mentions pepper and vinegar?** Oysters are often seasoned with pepper and vinegar before they are eaten.
8. **What does the poem teach the reader?** The poem suggests that it is wise to consider the instincts of our elders. The eldest oyster refuses to walk with the Carpenter and the Walrus. If the younger oysters had followed its lead, they would not have been eaten.

LESSON 3
1. **What is the title of the poem?** The title of the poem is "Christmas Greetings."
2. **What is the name of the poet who wrote "Christmas Greetings?"** The name of the poet is Lewis Carroll.
3. **What happens in the poem?** The poem narrator stops their trickery to wish a child a merry Christmas and a happy New Year.
4. **Who are the characters in the poem?** The poem characters are the fairy narrator, the lady, and the children.
5. **What does the poem teach the reader?** The poem reminds the reader to share peace and goodwill with others during the holiday season.

LESSON 4
1. **What is the title of the poem?** The title of the poem is "Beautiful Soup."
2. **What is the name of the poet who wrote "Beautiful Soup?"** The name of the poet is Lewis Carroll.
3. **What happens in the poem?** The narrator expresses his love for soup.
4. **Where does the poem take place?** Most likely indoors, in or near the kitchen or dining room.
5. **Who are the characters in the poem?** The only character is the narrator.
6. **What does the poem teach the reader?** The poem prompts the reader to enjoy and be thankful for their food.

ELEMENTARY POETRY VOLUME 3: POETRY OF NATURE, REVELRY, AND RHYME

LESSON 5
1. **What is the title of the poem?** The title of the poem is "A Life Lesson."
2. **What is the name of the poet who wrote "A Life Lesson?"** The name of the poet is James Whitcomb Riley.
3. **What happens in the poem?** A girl cries as she encounters difficulties. The narrator advises her to stop crying and reminds her that better days are ahead.
4. **Who are the characters in the poem?** The characters are the narrator and a little girl.
5. **What does the poem teach the reader?** The poem informs the reader that better days are often ahead.

LESSON 6
1. **What is the title of the poem?** The title of the poem is "The Raggedy Man."
2. **What is the name of the poet who wrote "The Raggedy Man?"** The name of the poet is James Whitcomb Riley.
3. **What happens in the poem?** A kind farm worker performs tasks around a farm such as feeding the animals, chopping wood, and working in the garden. He also climbs trees, picks apples, and plays horsey with the children.
4. **Where does the poem take place?** The poem takes place outdoors at a farm.
5. **Who are the characters in the poem?** The characters are Raggedy Man, the boy narrator, Pa, Elizabeth Ann, the hired girl on the narrator's farm, and the hired man on the Smoot farm.
6. **What does the poem teach the reader?** The poem suggests the reader respect hard work and kindness.

LESSON 7
1. **What is the title of the poem?** The title of the poem is "Little Orphant Annie."
2. **What is the name of the poet who wrote "Little Orphant Annie?"** The name of the poet is James Whitcomb Riley.
3. **What happens in the poem?** The poem introduces an orphan named Annie who tells tales of goblins that come for disobedient and greedy children.
4. **Where does the poem take place?** The poem takes place at the home of the young narrators hosting Little Orphant Annie.
5. **Who are the characters in the poem?** The characters include Annie, the young narrators listening to Annie's tales, the goblins, the naughty children, parents, teachers, and the needy.
6. **What does the poem teach the reader?** The poem reminds the reader to respect their parents and teachers and to be kind to the needy.

LESSON 8
1. **What is the title of the poem?** The title of the poem is "When the Frost is on the Punkin."
2. **What is the name of the poet who wrote "When the Frost is on the Punkin?"** The name of the poet is James Whitcomb Riley.
3. **What happens in the poem?** The poem celebrates the sights, sounds, sensations, and foods of farm life during fall.
4. **Where does the poem take place?** The poem takes place on a farm with pumpkins, corn, and animals.
5. **Who are the characters in the poem?** The characters are the narrator and the angelic women who bake delicious dishes using harvest foods.
6. **What does the poem teach the reader?** The poem reminds the reader to appreciate and celebrate the beauty of the fall season.

LESSON 9
1. **What is the title of the poem?** The title of the poem is "Hunting Weather."
2. **What is the name of the poet of "Hunting Weather?"** The name of the poet is Mary Austin.
3. **What happens in the poem?** The poem lists animal behaviors that signify the arrival of hunting weather.
4. **Where does the poem take place?** The poem takes place outside in various animal habitats.
5. **Who are the characters in the poem?** The characters are the narrator, the animals, and the hunters.
6. **What does the poem teach the reader?** The poem teaches us that animal behavior changes with the seasons.
7. **Per the poem, which animal behaviors signify the arrival of hunting weather?** The poem describes wild geese flying low, mallard drakes crying in the marshes, cattle moving down from high hills, and blackbirds grouping together as signs of hunting weather.

LESSON 10
1. **What is the title of the poem?** The title of the poem is "Signs of Spring."
2. **What is the name of the poet of "Signs of Spring?"** The name of the poet is Mary Austin.
3. **What happens in the poem?** The poem lists changes in plant and animal life that signify the arrival of spring.
4. **Where does the poem take place?** The poem takes place outside.
5. **Who are the characters in the poem?** The characters are the narrator and the animals.
6. **What does the poem teach the reader?** The poem teaches us that plants and animals change with the seasons.
7. **Per the poem, what are the signs of spring?** The poem describes flowers growing, blackbirds and sparrows in trees and bushes, budding orchard trees, green things growing, poppies blooming, and woolly clouds creeping.

LESSON 11
1. **What is the title of the poem?** The title of the poem is "The Sandhill Crane."
2. **What is the name of the poet of "The Sandhill Crane?"** The name of the poet is Mary Austin.
3. **What happens in the poem?** The poem describes how frogs and fishes scramble out of sight when the sandhill crane approaches.
4. **Where does the poem take place?** The poem takes place outdoors near water.
5. **Who are the characters in the poem?** The characters are the sandhill crane, frogs, and fishes.
6. **What does the poem teach the reader?** The poem teaches us that there are predators and prey in life.
7. **Why do the frogs and fishes hide from the sandhill crane?** The frogs and fishes fear they will be eaten by the sandhill crane.

LESSON 12
1. **What is the title of the poem?** The title of the poem is "Blue-Eyed Grass."
2. **What is the name of the poet of "Blue-Eyed Grass?"** The name of the poet is Mary Austin.
3. **What happens in the poem?** The poem describes the sights and sounds of the arrival of summer.
4. **Where does the poem take place?** The poem takes place outside.
5. **What does the poem teach the reader?** The poem teaches us some sights and sounds of summer.
6. **Per the poem, what are the signs that summer has arrived?** The signs that summer has arrived include the appearance of blooming flowers such as blue-eyed grass and yarrow, plants such as cattails and milkweeds, and animals such as linnets, blackbirds, and bees.

LESSON 13
1. **What is the title of the poem?** The title of the poem is "Prairie-Dog Town."
2. **What is the name of the poet who wrote "Prairie-Dog Town?"** The name of the poet is Mary Austin.
3. **What happens in the poem?** Peter Prairie-Dog builds an underground home in Prairie-Dog Town.
4. **Where does the poem take place?** The poem takes place outside at Prairie-Dog Town.
5. **Who are the characters in the poem?** The characters are the narrator and Peter Prairie-Dog.
6. **What does the poem teach the reader?** The poem teaches us that prairie dogs live in burrows under the ground. They often live together in large towns.
7. **What does Peter Prairie-Dog do when he sees anyone above ground?** When Peter Prairie-Dog sees anyone above ground, he stands still like a stick.

LESSON 14
1. **What is the title of the poem?** The title of the poem is "Wynken, Blynken, and Nod."
2. **What is the name of the poet who wrote "Wynken, Blynken, and Nod?"** The name of the poet is Eugene Field.
3. **What happens in the poem?** Wynken, Blynken, and Nod ride in a wooden shoe to fish in a beautiful sea. The poem reveals Wynken and Blynken are the eyes of a sleeping child, Nod is the child's head, and the wooden shoe is the child's bed.
4. **Where does the poem take place?** The poem takes place in a child's bedroom and a dream world.
5. **Who are the characters in the poem?** The character is a child (and the child's Wynken, Blynken, and Nod).
6. **What does the poem teach the reader?** The poem suggests that we can have magical, wondrous dreams as we sleep.

LESSON 15
1. **What is the title of the poem?** The title of the poem is "Little Blue Pigeon."
2. **What is the name of the poet who wrote "Little Blue Pigeon?"** The name of the poet is Eugene Field.
3. **What happens in the poem?** The lullaby poem describes the beauty of the night and encourages children to sleep.
4. **Where does the poem take place?** The poem most likely takes place in a child's bedroom.
5. **Who are the characters in the poem?** The characters include the little pigeon (child) and the narrator (parent or another person singing the child to sleep).
6. **What does the poem teach the reader?** The poem provides a lullaby that can be used to help children relax and fall sleep.

LESSON 16
1. **What is the title of the poem?** The title of the poem is "The Sugar Plum Tree."
2. **What is the name of the poet who wrote "The Sugar Plum Tree?"** The name of the poet is Eugene Field.
3. **What happens in the poem?** The lovely Sugar-Plum Tree grows delicious sweets that make children happy. Children must enlist the help of the chocolate cat and gingerbread dog to get the candy.
4. **Where does the poem take place?** The poem takes place in the garden of Shut-Eye Town on the shore of the Lollypop sea.
5. **Who are the characters in the poem?** The characters are the children, the chocolate cat, the gingerbread dog, and the narrator.
6. **What does the poem teach the reader?** The poem suggests the reader be creative and enlist the help of others to achieve a goal.

LESSON 17
1. **What is the title of the poem?** The title of the poem is "The Duel."
2. **What is the name of the poet who wrote "The Duel?"** The name of the poet is Eugene Field.
3. **What happens in the poem?** A gingham dog and a calico cat fight a battle that they both lose.
4. **Where does the poem take place?** The poem most likely takes place in a house or other building.
5. **Who are the characters in the poem?** The characters are the gingham dog, the calico cat, the narrator, an old Dutch clock, a Chinese plate, and gossiping folks.
6. **What does the poem teach the reader?** The poem teaches the reader that some battles are senseless and not worth fighting - for no one wins.

LESSON 18
1. **What is the title of the poem?** The title of the poem is "Jest 'Fore Christmas."
2. **What is the name of the poet who wrote "Jest 'Fore Christmas?"** The name of the poet is Eugene Field.
3. **What happens in the poem?** A mischievous boy stops his troublemaking ways right before Christmas to ensure he receives presents.
4. **Who are the characters in the poem?** The characters include the boy narrator, his friends, his mother, his father, his dog, his grandmother, and the grocery man.
5. **What does the poem teach the reader?** The poem teaches the reader that people may temporarily change their behavior to get what they want.

LESSON 19
1. **What is the title of the poem?** The title of the poem is "Fifteen Men on the Dead Man's Chest."
2. **What is the name of the poet who wrote "Fifteen Men on the Dead Man's Chest?"** The name of the poet is Robert Louis Stevenson.
3. **What happens in the poem?** The poem describes the fates of the men marooned by the pirate Blackbeard on Dead Man's Chest island.
4. **Where does the poem take place?** The poem takes place on Dead Man's Chest island.
5. **Who are the characters in the poem?** The characters are the narrator, the marooned men who survived, and those who perished on Dead Man's Chest island.

LESSON 20
1. **What is the title of the poem?** The title of the poem is "A Good Boy."
2. **What is the name of the poet who wrote "A Good Boy?"** The name of the poet is Robert Louis Stevenson.
3. **What happens in the poem?** The poem describes a day in the life of a happy boy.
4. **Where does the poem take place?** The poem takes place in the places the boy visits, from where he plays to where he sleeps.
5. **Who are the characters in the poem?** The sole character is the good boy, the narrator of the poem.
6. **What does the poem teach the reader?** To poem reminds the reader to have a happy, optimistic mindset and be thankful for what we have.

LESSON 21
1. **What is the title of the poem?** The title of the poem is "Windy Nights."
2. **What is the name of the poet who wrote "Windy Nights?"** The name of the poet is Robert Louis Stevenson.
3. **What happens in the poem?** The poem describes a man galloping back and forth during the night.
4. **Who are the characters in the poem?** The characters are the narrator and the man riding the horse.
5. **What does the poem teach the reader?** The poem reminds the reader that there are intriguing mysteries all around us.

LESSON 22
1. **What is the title of the poem?** The title of the poem is "The Swing."
2. **What is the name of the poet who wrote "The Swing?"** The name of the poet is Robert Louis Stevenson.
3. **What happens in the poem?** The poem describes the feelings and sights experienced when swinging through the air.
4. **Who are the characters in the poem?** The only character is the swinging narrator.
5. **What does the poem teach the reader?** The poem reminds the reader to enjoy life's simple pleasures, such as enjoying fresh air and the sights of the countryside.

LESSON 23
1. **What is the title of the poem?** The title of the poem is "My Shadow."
2. **What is the name of the poet who wrote "My Shadow?"** The name of the poet is Robert Louis Stevenson.
3. **What happens in the poem?** The poem describes a child's observations of their shadow, which changes throughout the day and night.
4. **Who are the characters in the poem?** The characters are the narrator and their shadow.
5. **What does the poem teach the reader?** The poem communicates how the shape and size of shadows are dependent upon the time of day/night (e.g. the angle and positioning of a light source such as the sun).

LESSON 24
1. **What is the title of the poem?** The title of the poem is "Solitude."
2. **What is the name of the poet who wrote "Solitude?"** The name of the poet is Ella Wheeler Wilcox.
3. **What happens in the poem?** The poem states people tend to flock to those who are happy and shun those who are sad.
4. **Who are the characters in the poem?** The characters are the narrator and the rest of the world.
5. **What does the poem teach the reader?** The poem states that some people are fair-weather friends that disappear when our lives become difficult.

LESSON 25
1. **What is the title of the poem?** The title of the poem is "A Fable."
2. **What is the name of the poet who wrote "A Fable?"** The name of the poet is Ella Wheeler Wilcox.
3. **What happens in the poem?** An eagle ignores a gossiping group of birds who dislike how high the eagle flies.
4. **Who are the characters in the poem?** The main characters include the caucus of birds and the eagle.
5. **What does the poem teach the reader?** The poem suggests that, like the eagle, the reader should ignore small-minded gossip and jealousy and focus on achieving their goals.

LESSON 26
1. **What is the title of the poem?** The title of the poem is "Sunset."
2. **What is the name of the poet who wrote "Sunset?"** The name of the poet is Ella Wheeler Wilcox.
3. **What happens in the poem?** Day lowers a lamp (the sun) over the edge of the world (the horizon) at sunset.
4. **Who are the characters in the poem?** The characters are the narrator and "day."
5. **What does the poem teach the reader?** The poem serves as an example of personification, treating the "day" as if it were a person holding a lamp.

LESSON 27
1. **What is the title of the poem?** The title of the poem is "A March Snow."
2. **What is the name of the poet who wrote "A March Snow?"** The name of the poet is Ella Wheeler Wilcox.
3. **What happens in the poem?** The narrator compares a white sheet of new snow covering dirty snow to a white sheet of repentance covering our past mistakes.
4. **Who are the characters in the poem?** The poem character is the narrator.
5. **What does the poem teach the reader?** The poem reminds the reader that they can renew themselves, even in the face of past mistakes.

LESSON 28
1. **What is the title of the poem?** The title of the poem is "The Fisherman."
2. **What is the name of the poet who wrote "The Fisherman?"** The name of the poet is Abbie Farwell Brown.
3. **What happens in the poem?** The poem describes a fisherman with curious eyes who lives partly on the shore and partly on the sea.
4. **Who are the characters in the poem?** The characters are the narrator and the fisherman.
5. **What does a fisherman do for a living?** A fisherman catches and sells fish and other sea creatures for human consumption.
6. **How is the fisherman from the poem different from many other people?** The fisherman starts work while others are still sleeping. He lives half upon the sea, has curious eyes, tells wondrous tales, and disdains city life.

LESSON 29
1. **What is the title of the poem?** The title of the poem is "Friends."
2. **What is the name of the poet who wrote "Friends?"** The name of the poet is Abbie Farwell Brown.
3. **What happens in the poem?** The narrator describes their Friends - the Sky, the Sunshine, and the Wind.
4. **Who are the characters in the poem?** The characters are the narrator, the Sky, the Sunshine, and the Wind.
5. **Do you believe the Sky, the Sunshine, and the Wind can truly be our friends?** What about animals? Why or why not? Answers vary. One definition of friends might include the criterion of "mutual affection." Can the Sky show us affection? Can an animal show us affection?

LESSON 30
1. **What is the title of the poem?** The title of the poem is "The Faithless Flowers."
2. **What is the name of the poet who wrote "The Faithless Flowers?"** The name of the poet is Abbie Farwell Brown.
3. **What happens in the poem?** The narrator wonders why flowers don't live up to their names.
4. **Who are the characters in the poem?** The only character is the narrator.

LESSON 31
1. **What is the title of the poem?** The title of the poem is "Baby's Valentine."
2. **What is the name of the poet who wrote "Baby's Valentine?"** The name of the poet is Abbie Farwell Brown.
3. **What happens in the poem?** The narrator describes their love and adoration of a baby.
4. **Who are the characters in the poem?** The characters are the narrator, the baby, and the animals that will pay homage to the baby.

LESSON 32
1. **What is the title of the poem?** The title of the poem is "A Tryst."
2. **What is the name of the poet who wrote "A Tryst?"** The name of the poet is Abbie Farwell Brown.
3. **What happens in the poem?** The narrator promises to meet the sun at dawn the following day, watches the sun set, and goes to bed.
4. **Who are the characters in the poem?** The characters are the narrator and the sun.

LESSON 33
1. **What is the title of the poem?** The title of the poem is "There Will Come Soft Rains."
2. **What is the name of the poet who wrote "There Will Come Soft Rains?"** The name of the poet is Sara Teasdale.
3. **What happens in the poem?** The poem ponders the significance of mankind to the rain, the animals, the plants, and the passing seasons.
4. **Who are the characters in the poem?** The characters are the narrator, the rest of mankind, the plants, the animals, the seasons, and the rain.
5. **Which scents does the poem describe?** The poem mentions the smell of the ground when the rains come.
6. **Which sounds does the poem describe?** The poem describes the sounds of swallows circling, frogs singing at night, and robins whistling.

LESSON 34
1. **What is the title of the poem?** The title of the poem is "Barter."
2. **What is the name of the poet who wrote "Barter?"** The name of the poet is Sara Teasdale.
3. **What happens in the poem?** The poem advises us to spend all we have on the loveliness and peace life is selling.
4. **Who are the characters in the poem?** The characters are the narrator, the reader (you), children, and life.
5. **The title of the poem is "Barter." What must we give to life in exchange for the things life has to sell?** We must give life our time, our attention, and at times all we have been, or could be.
6. **What does life have to sell?** The poem mentions blue waves, soaring fire, children's wonder, music, the scent of pine trees, eyes that love, arms that hold, and peace.

LESSON 35
1. **What is the title of the poem?** The title of the poem is "Let It Be Forgotten."
2. **What is the name of the poet who wrote "Let It Be Forgotten?"** The name of the poet is Sara Teasdale.
3. **What happens in the poem?** The poem asks that something be forgotten like faded flowers, extinguished fires, or the sound of a footstep in a long ago melted snow.
4. **Who are the characters in the poem?** The character is the narrator.
5. **What was once "singing gold" in the poem?** A forgotten fire was once "singing gold."

LESSON 36
1. **What is the title of the poem?** The title of the poem is "Wishes."
2. **What is the name of the poet who wrote "Wishes?"** The name of the poet is Sara Teasdale.
3. **What happens in the poem?** The child narrator enjoys wishing for a kitty and a blue balloon, despite knowing their wishes will probably not come true.
4. **Who are the characters in the poem?** The human characters are the child narrator and her nursie.
5. **Do you think it is worthwhile to wish for things that will likely never come true?** Answers vary.

REFERENCES AND ADDITIONAL READING

1. **Lewis Carrol**
   a. ***Lewis Carroll Portrait*** **(1863, {PD-US})**
      i. Source: https://commons.wikimedia.org/wiki/File:Lewis_Carroll_1863.jpg
      ii. License: The author died in 1875, so this work is in the public domain in its country of origin and other countries and areas where the copyright term is the author's life plus 100 years or less. This work is in the public domain in the United States because it was published (or registered with the U.S. Copyright Office) before January 1, 1923.
   b. ***Map of Europe*** **({PD-US})**
      i. Source: https://commons.wikimedia.org/wiki/File:Europe_geopolitical_map_of_Europe.jpg
      ii. License: This work has been released into the public domain by its author, *Public Domain Images*. This applies worldwide. *Public Domain Images* grants anyone the right to use this work for any purpose, without any conditions, unless such conditions are required by law.
   c. **"*How Doth the Little Crocodile*" (1866, {PD-US})**
      i. Carroll, L. (1866). "Alice's Adventures in Wonderland". London: Macmillan and Co.
      ii. License: The author died in 1898, so this work is in the public domain in its country of origin and other countries and areas where the copyright term is the author's life plus 100 years or less. This work is in the public domain in the United States because it was published (or registered with the U.S. Copyright Office) before January 1, 1923.
   d. ***Map of Egypt*** **({PD-US})**
      i. Source: http://ian.macky.net/pat/map/eg/eg_blu.gif
      ii. License: This work has been released into the public domain by its author, Ian Macky. This applies worldwide. Ian Macky grants anyone the right to use this work for any purpose, without any conditions, unless such conditions are required by law.
   e. **"*The Walrus and The Carpenter*" (1871, {PD-US})**
      i. Carroll, C. (1871). "Through the Looking Glass". London: Macmillan.
      ii. License: The author died in 1898, so this work is in the public domain in its country of origin and other countries and areas where the copyright term is the author's life plus 100 years or less. This work is in the public domain in the United States because it was published (or registered with the U.S. Copyright Office) before January 1, 1923.
   f. **"*The Walrus and the Carpenter*" Illustrations (1902, {PD-US})**
      i. Carroll, C. and Newell, P. (1902). "Through the looking glass and what Alice found there". New York and London : Harper & Bros.
      ii. License: This work is in the public domain in the United States because it was published (or registered with the U.S. Copyright Office) before January 1, 1923. This work is in the public domain in the United States because it was published (or registered with the U.S. Copyright Office) before January 1, 1923.
   g. Lewis Carroll. Wikipedia. Wikipedia.org. n.p.

2. **James Whitcomb Riley**
   a. ***James Whitcomb Riley Portrait*** **(1913, {PD-US})**
      i. Source: https://commons.wikimedia.org/wiki/File:James_Whitcomb_Riley,_1913.jpg
      ii. License: This media file is in the public domain in the United States. This applies to U.S. works where the copyright has expired, often because its first publication occurred prior to January 1, 1923.
   b. ***Map of the United States*** **({PD-US})**
      i. Source: https://commons.wikimedia.org/wiki/File:United_States_Public_Domain_Map.svg
      ii. License: This image is a work of a United States Department of Justice employee, taken or made as part of that person's official duties. As a work of the U.S. federal government, the image is in the public domain (17 U.S.C. § 101 and 105).

c. *"A Life Lesson"* (1904, {PD-US})
   i. Bliss, C. (Editor) (1904). "The World's Best Poetry, edited by Bliss Carman, et al.." Philadelphia: John D. Morris & Co.
   ii. License: The author died in 1916, so this work is in the public domain in its country of origin and other countries and areas where the copyright term is the author's life plus 100 years or less. This work is in the public domain in the United States because it was published (or registered with the U.S. Copyright Office) before January 1, 1923.
d. *"The Raggedy Man"* (1888, {PD-US})
   i. Wilder, M. (Editor) (1904). "The Wit and Humor of America." New York and London: Funk & Wagnalls Company.
   ii. License: The author died in 1916, so this work is in the public domain in its country of origin and other countries and areas where the copyright term is the author's life plus 100 years or less. This work is in the public domain in the United States because it was published (or registered with the U.S. Copyright Office) before January 1, 1923.
e. **The Raggedy Man Image (1916, {PD-US})**
   i. Riley, J. (1916). "James Whitcomb Riley's Complete Works." New York and Indianapolis: The Bobbs-Merrill Company.
   ii. License: The author died in 1916, so this work is in the public domain in its country of origin and other countries and areas where the copyright term is the author's life plus 100 years or less. This work is in the public domain in the United States because it was published (or registered with the U.S. Copyright Office) before January 1, 1923.
f. *"Little Orphant Annie"* (1885, {PD-US})
   i. Riley, J (1885). " The Coo-ee Reciter." London, Melbourne & Toronto: Ward, Lock & Co. Limited.
   ii. License: The author died in 1916, so this work is in the public domain in its country of origin and other countries and areas where the copyright term is the author's life plus 100 years or less. This work is in the public domain in the United States because it was published (or registered with the U.S. Copyright Office) before January 1, 1923.
g. *"When the Frost is on the Punkin"* (**1883**, {PD-US})
   i. Riley, J. (**1883**). "Riley Farm-Rhymes." New York: Grosset & Dunlap.
   ii. License: The author died in 1916, so this work is in the public domain in its country of origin and other countries and areas where the copyright term is the author's life plus 100 years or less. This work is in the public domain in the United States because it was published (or registered with the U.S. Copyright Office) before January 1, 1923.
h. *Little Orphant Allie Portrait* (1863, {PD-US})
   i. Source: https://commons.wikimedia.org/wiki/File:Mary_Allice_Smith,_c_1863.jpg
   ii. License: This media file is in the public domain in the United States. This applies to U.S. works where the copyright has expired, often because its first publication occurred prior to January 1, 1923.
i. James Whitcomb Riley. Wikipedia. Wikipedia.org. n.p.

3. **Mary Austin**
   a. *Mary Hunter Austin Portrait* (**No later than 1912, {PD-US}**)
      i. Source: https://commons.wikimedia.org/wiki/File:Picture_of_Mary_Austin.jpg
      ii. License: This media file is in the public domain in the United States. This applies to U.S. works where the copyright has expired, often because its first publication occurred prior to January 1, 1923.
   b. *"Hunting Weather"* (1903, {PD-US})
      i. Dodge, M. (Editor) (1903). "St. Nicholas, Volume 30, Part 2." New York: The Century Co.
      ii. License: This work is in the public domain in the United States because it was published (or registered with the U.S. Copyright Office) before January 1, 1923.

c. *"Signs of Spring"* (1903, {PD-US})
   i. Dodge, M. (Editor) (1903). "St. Nicholas, Volume 30, Part 1." New York: The Century Co.
   ii. License: This work is in the public domain in the United States because it was published (or registered with the U.S. Copyright Office) before January 1, 1923.
d. *"The Sandhill Crane"* (1916, {PD-US})
   i. Austin, M. (1916). "Pacific Rural Press (Magazine)."
   ii. License: This work is in the public domain in the United States because it was published (or registered with the U.S. Copyright Office) before January 1, 1923.
e. *"Blue-Eyed Grass"* (1904, {PD-US})
   i. Austin, M. (1904). "St. Nicholas (Magazine)."
   ii. License: This work is in the public domain in the United States because it was published (or registered with the U.S. Copyright Office) before January 1, 1923.
f. Mary Austin. Wikipedia. Wikipedia.org. n.p.

4. **Eugene Field**
   a. *Eugene Field Portrait* (1914, {PD-US})
      i. Source: https://commons.wikimedia.org/wiki/File:NSRW_Eugene_Field.jpg (*The New Student's Reference Work* Published 1914)
      ii. License: This media file is in the public domain in the United States. This applies to U.S. works where the copyright has expired, often because its first publication occurred prior to January 1, 1923.
   b. *"Wynken, Blynken, and Nod"* (1895, {PD-US})
      i. Edmund Clarence Stedman, ed. (1895). "An American Anthology." Boston: Houghton Mifflin.
      ii. License: The author died in 1895, so this work is in the public domain in its country of origin and other countries and areas where the copyright term is the author's life plus 100 years or less. This work is in the public domain in the United States because it was published (or registered with the U.S. Copyright Office) before January 1, 1923.
   c. *Wynken, Blynken, and Nod Image* (1907, {PD-US})
      i. Louey, C. and Dibdin S. (1907). "The Golden Staircase - Poems and Verses for Children." New York: G.P. Putnam's Sons.
      ii. License: This work is in the public domain in the United States because it was published (or registered with the U.S. Copyright Office) before January 1, 1923.
   d. *"Little Blue Pigeon (Japanese Lullaby)"* (1904, {PD-US})
      i. The World's Best Poetry, ed. by Bliss Carman, et al. Philadelphia: John D. Morris & Co., 1904."
      ii. License: The author died in 1895, so this work is in the public domain in its country of origin and other countries and areas where the copyright term is the author's life plus 100 years or less. This work is in the public domain in the United States because it was published (or registered with the U.S. Copyright Office) before January 1, 1923.
   e. *Little Blue Pigeon in Bed Image* (1904, {PD-US})
      i. Field, E. Illustrated by Robinson C. (1904). "Lullaby Land". New York. Charles Scribner's Sons.
      ii. License: This work is in the public domain in the United States because it was published (or registered with the U.S. Copyright Office) before January 1, 1923.
   f. *"The Sugar Plum Tree"* (1904, {PD-US})
      i. Field, E. Illustrated by Robinson C. (1904). "Lullaby Land". New York. Charles Scribner's Sons.
      ii. License: The author died in 1895, so this work is in the public domain in its country of origin and other countries and areas where the copyright term is the author's life plus 100 years or

less. This work is in the public domain in the United States because it was published (or registered with the U.S. Copyright Office) before January 1, 1923.

- g. *"The Duel"* (1912, {PD-US})
    - i. Lounsbury, Thomas R., ed. Yale Book of American Verse. New Haven: Yale University Press, 1912.
    - ii. License: The author died in 1895, so this work is in the public domain in its country of origin and other countries and areas where the copyright term is the author's life plus 100 years or less. This work is in the public domain in the United States because it was published (or registered with the U.S. Copyright Office) before January 1, 1923.
- h. *"Jest 'Fore Christmas"* (1904, {PD-US})
    - i. Field, E. "Poems of Childhood." New York: Charles Scribner's Sons.
    - ii. License: The author died in 1895, so this work is in the public domain in its country of origin and other countries and areas where the copyright term is the author's life plus 100 years or less. This work is in the public domain in the United States because it was published (or registered with the U.S. Copyright Office) before January 1, 1923.
- i. *Map of Asia (Including Sri Lanka)* (CC0, {PD-US})
    - i. Source: www.wpclipart.com/geography/Country_Maps/I/India/India_map_location_label.png.html
    - ii. License: This work has been released into the public domain by its author. This applies worldwide. Public Domain Images grants anyone the right to use this work for any purpose, without any conditions, unless such conditions are required by law.
- j. *Buffalo Bill's Wild Wild West Show Poster* (1899, {PD-US})
    - i. Source: https://en.wikipedia.org/wiki/File:Buffalo_bill_wild_west_show_c1899.jpg
    - ii. License: This work is in the public domain in the United States because it was published (or registered with the U.S. Copyright Office) before January 1, 1923.
- k. Eugene Field. Wikipedia. Wikipedia.org. n.p.

5. **Robert Louis Stevenson**
    - a. *Robert Louis Stevenson Portrait* (1893, {PD-US})
        - i. Source: https://commons.wikimedia.org/wiki/File:Portrait_of_Robert_Louis_Stevenson.jpg
        - ii. License: This work is in the public domain in the United States because it was published (or registered with the U.S. Copyright Office) before January 1, 1923. The author died in 1934, so this work is in the public domain in its country of origin and other countries and areas where the copyright term is the author's life plus 80 years or less.
    - b. *"Fifteen Men on the Dead Man's Chest"* (1882, {PD-US})
        - i. Stevenson, R.L. "Treasure Island. (1882)" London: Cassell.
        - ii. License: The author died in 1894, so this work is in the public domain in its country of origin and other countries and areas where the copyright term is the author's life plus 100 years or less. This work is in the public domain in the United States because it was published (or registered with the U.S. Copyright Office) before January 1, 1923.
    - c. *CIA Map of the Caribbean* (CC0, {PD-US})
        - i. Source: https://commons.wikimedia.org/wiki/File:CIA_map_of_the_Caribbean.png
        - ii. License: This image is in the public domain because it contains materials that originally came from the United States Central Intelligence Agency's World Factbook.
    - d. *"A Good Boy"* (1905, {PD-US})
        - i. Stevenson, R.L. "A Child's Garden of Verses. (1905)" New York: Charles Scribner's Sons.
        - ii. License: See 5b.
    - e. *"Windy Nights"* (1882, {PD-US})
        - i. Stevenson, R.L. "A Child's Garden of Verses. (1905)" New York: Charles Scribner's Sons.

ii. License: The author died in 1894, so this work is in the public domain in its country of origin and other countries and areas where the copyright term is the author's life plus 100 years or less. This work is in the public domain in the United States because it was published (or registered with the U.S. Copyright Office) before January 1, 1923.
   f. *"The Swing"* (1882, {PD-US})
      i. Stevenson, R.L. "A Child's Garden of Verses. (1905)" New York: Charles Scribner's Sons.
      ii. License: The author died in 1894, so this work is in the public domain in its country of origin and other countries and areas where the copyright term is the author's life plus 100 years or less. This work is in the public domain in the United States because it was published (or registered with the U.S. Copyright Office) before January 1, 1923.
   g. Robert Louis Stevenson. Wikipedia. Wikipedia.org. n.p.
6. **Ella Wheeler Wilcox**
   a. *Ella Wheeler Wilcox Portrait* (1919, {PD-US})
      i. Source: https://commons.wikimedia.org/wiki/File:Ella_Wheeler_Wilcox_circa_1919.jpg
      ii. License: This work is in the public domain in the United States because it was published (or registered with the U.S. Copyright Office) before January 1, 1923.
   b. Ella Wheeler Wilcox. Wikipedia. Wikipedia.org. n.p.
7. **Abbie Farwell Brown**
   a. *Fisherman Image* (CC0, {PD-US})
      i. Source: https://pixabay.com/en/fish-fisherman-fishing-line-man-30826/
      ii. License: This work has been released into the public domain by its author. This applies worldwide. Public Domain Images grants anyone the right to use this work for any purpose, without any conditions, unless such conditions are required by law.
   b. Abbie Farwell Brown. Wikipedia. Wikipedia.org. n.p.
8. **Sara Teasdale**
   a. *Sara Teasdale Portrait* (1919, {PD-US})
      i. Source: https://commons.wikimedia.org/wiki/File:Ella_Wheeler_Wilcox_circa_1919.jpg
      ii. License: This work is in the public domain in the United States because it was published (or registered with the U.S. Copyright Office) before January 1, 1923.
   b. Sara Teasdale. Wikipedia. Wikipedia.org. n.p.
9. *All Other Clipart and Images.* Open Clipart. openclipart.org. n.p. ({PD-US})
10. *All Definitions.* Wiktionary: Public Domain Sources. en.wiktionary.org. n.p. ({PD-US})

ABOUT THE AUTHOR

Sonja Glumich is a scientist, educator, wife, and mother who is inspired by Charlotte Mason's living works approach to homeschooling. She is the founder of Under the Home (underthehome.org), an online homeschool curriculum featuring low-cost courses in art history, poetry, prose, music, history, science, studio art, mathematics, reading, and Shakespeare. Sonja's husband, Chris, homeschools their three school-aged children using the Under the Home curriculum as featured in this book.

Sonja graduated magna cum laude with bachelor's degrees in biology, chemistry, and computer science and later earned a master's degree in information technology. She has also completed education classes and student teaching leading to certification to teach secondary science.

Sonja has experience teaching students of all ages, from preschool to graduate school, including as a middle school and high school science public school teacher. She has also served as an Adjunct Professor for Syracuse University and co-created two graduate-level cyber courses. She currently works as a computer scientist for the Air Force Research Laboratory. Her current research and education interests are security systems engineering, cyber vulnerability assessments, and everything homeschooling.

www.ingramcontent.com/pod-product-compliance
Lightning Source LLC
LaVergne TN
LVHW081357060426
835510LV00016B/1879

9 781948 783019